GREAT
ESCAPES

Escapes from Religious Oppression

Stephen Currie

LUCENT
BOOKS®

THOMSON

GALE

200.9
CUR

San Diego • Detroit • New York • San Francisco • Cleveland • New Haven, Conn. • Waterville, Maine • London • Munich

THOMSON

─────── ✦ ───────™

GALE

© 2004 by Lucent Books. Lucent Books is an imprint of The Gale Group, Inc.,
a division of Thomson Learning, Inc.

Lucent Books® and Thomson Learning™ are trademarks used herein under license.

For more information, contact
Lucent Books
27500 Drake Rd.
Farmington Hills, MI 48331-3535
Or you can visit our Internet site at http://www.gale.com

LIBRARY OF CONGRESS CATALOGING-IN-PUBLICATION DATA

Currie, Stephen, 1960–
    Escapes from religious oppression / by Stephen Currie.
        p. cm. — (Great escapes)
Summary: Describes five escapes from religious oppression, from three continents in three
centuries, of individuals or groups representing five different faiths who were willing to
risk everything they had for the chance to worship freely.
Includes bibliographical references and index.
    ISBN 1-59018-280-4 (alk. paper)
    1. Freedom of religion—Biography—Juvenile literature. 2. Human rights—Biography—
Juvenile literature. 3. Persecution—Biography—Juvenile literature. 4. Religious tolerance—
Biography—Juvenile literature. [1. Religious leaders. 2. Freedom of religion. 3. Persecution.]
I. Title. II. Series.
BL640.C87 2004
200'.9—dc22

                                                                            2003016268

Printed in the United States of America

Contents

Foreword

THE NOTION OF escape strikes a chord in most of us. We are intrigued by tales of narrow deliverance from adversity and delight in the stories of those who have successfully skirted disaster. When a few seemingly chosen people are liberated from a fate that befalls many others, we feel that to some degree the larger injustice has been rectified; that in their freedom, a small bit of justice prevailed.

Persecution and disaster, whether in nature or from what has frequently been called "man's inhumanity to man," have been all too common throughout history. Fires, floods, and earthquakes have killed millions; enslavement, inquisitions, and so-called ethnic cleansing millions more. Time and again, people have faced what seems to be certain death and looked for a way out. The stories of these escapes reveal the emotional and physical strength of our fellow human beings. They are at once dramatic, compelling, and inspirational.

Some of these escapes have been entirely the work of one brave person. Others have involved hundreds or even thousands of people. Escapees themselves vary; some seek to return to a life they have lost, others flee to a life they have only dreamed of, still others are simply fugitives against time. Their stories enlighten even the darkest events of history, making it clear that wherever there is determination, courage, and creativity, there is hope. Dr. Viktor E. Frankl, a survivor of four Nazi concentration camps, expressed this tenacity in the following way: "Everything can be taken from a man but one thing: the last of human freedoms—to choose one's attitude in any given set of circumstances—to choose one's own way."

People who are mired in captivity become willing to chance the unknown at any cost. Americans who escaped from slavery, for example, escaped toward a vision that the life they had never been allowed to live would offer them new hope. Fugitive slaves had no inkling of what life in free territory would hold for them, or if they would even make it there alive. Fears of the unknown, however, were outweighed by the mere possibility of living a free life.

While many escapes involve careful and intricate planning, no path of flight follows a fixed blueprint. Most escapes owe their success to on-the-spot improvisation and keen resourcefulness. A piece of clothing found at a critical juncture might be just the thing out of which to fashion a cunning disguise; a brick lying harmlessly in the corner of a room might provide just enough support to boost a person through the crack in a window.

Conversely, fate may carelessly toss many pitfalls at the feet of those in flight. An unexpected flood might render a road impassable; a sympathetic train conductor might be suddenly fired, replaced with an unfriendly stranger. All escapes are both hindered and helped by such blind chance. Those fleeing for their lives must be nimble enough to dodge obstacles and snatch at opportunities that might affect their chances along the way.

It is common for people who have undergone such ordeals to question whether their salvation came to them by chance, or if they were somehow chosen for a greater scheme, a larger purpose. All become changed people, bestowed with a grand sense of purpose and a rich appreciation for life. It is this appreciation for life too that draws us to their stories, as they impress upon us the importance of living every day to its fullest, and inspire us to find ways to escape from our own prisons.

Lucent's Great Escapes series describes some of the most remarkable escapes in history. Each volume chronicles five individual stories on a common topic. The narratives focus on planning, executing, and surviving the escapes. The books quote liberally from primary sources, while ample background information lends historical context. An appendix of primary sources is also included in each volume, sharing additional stories of escape not profiled in the main text. Endnotes, two bibliographies, maps of escape routes, and sidebars enhance each volume.

Introduction

Religion and Intolerance

THE STORY OF humanity is full of religious prejudice. Since the beginning of recorded history, and probably long before, people have oppressed those who worshiped gods different from theirs—or, often, those who worshiped the same gods in different ways.

Religious prejudice can take several different forms. Sometimes the members of one powerful religious group simply refuse to permit those of other faiths to worship as they please. Sometimes, especially if the groups are more or less evenly matched in numbers and strength, physical violence can break out between people from different religions. In the nations of India, Pakistan, and Bangladesh, for example, Hindus and Muslims have battled for many years over their religious differences.

Sadly, religious prejudice many times ends with the murder of those who profess another religion. Most notably, that took place in Nazi Germany during and just before World War II. Under the leadership of the fascist dictator Adolf Hitler, the Nazis murdered about 6 million Jews out of an irrational and vicious hatred for their religion. The Nazis also executed many Christians whose religious beliefs caused them to oppose the Nazi activities.

Religious prejudice can be aimed at any faith and used as a weapon by almost any group. Intolerance can appear even when groups share the basics of belief and practice. For several centuries, for example, the Protestants and the Roman Catholics of Northern Ireland have argued and fought, although both sides worship the same Christian God. Even the absence of religion can spark oppression. Some atheists do not feel fully tolerated in the United States today, and the problem has been worse at certain times in the past. The twentieth century has also seen the rise of officially atheist Communist governments, many strongly opposed to spirituality in all its forms. Some of the worst religious oppression in recent years has been inflicted by these antireligious states.

Escape

Even when religious intolerance is relatively mild, it is still oppressive and unfair. But unless the members of a persecuted group have the strength and resources to fight back, which many do not, they have few options. In a reasonably democratic country, they can appeal to the legal system; in a less open society, they can try to win the sympathy and attention of the leaders. But such measures, throughout history, have seldom been successful. For

Hooded Protestants armed with guns in Belfast, Northern Ireland, prepare to disperse a group of Catholics demonstrating against a Protestant parade.

Religion and Politics

It can often be difficult to distinguish religious oppression from persecution based on ethnic, racial, or political differences. Much of the time, in fact, religious intolerance goes hand in hand with political conflict. The arguments between India and Pakistan have not been simply about the Hindu and Muslim religions, any more than strife in the Middle East is based purely on a spiritual disagreement between Muslims and Jews. Though religious oppression is present in both cases, these conflicts are also about the political issue of who shall control territory.

Each of the escape stories in this book reflects not only a religious disagreement, but a political clash as well. The political power wielded by the early Mormons, for instance, helped turn their neighbors against them. Likewise, the Christian Serbs of Bosnia were determined not to cede governmental authority to their Muslim neighbors. Religious differences between groups, however, tend to crop up long before political issues begin to surface, and most often, they serve as the engine that drives oppression. Had the Mormons not already drawn the attention of their neighbors for their religious beliefs, it is doubtful that they would have been so despised by their enemies. And if there had not been a religious difference between the Christians and the Muslims of Bosnia, then the disastrous political disagreements in the area might never have broken out at all. As a very general rule, political differences add to the existing religious conflicts, not the other way around.

many of the oppressed, then, the only answer has been to escape—to find a place where they can worship according to the dictates of their conscience.

Like religious oppression itself, escapes from religious persecution defy easy classification. Some escapes are undertaken by just one person or by a small group, while others are mass migrations of hundreds or even thousands of people seeking a refuge. The people who attempt escape may not be in any immediate physical danger, or they may be fleeing imprisonment, torture, even execution. The escapes themselves can be short, quick, and relatively simple, or they can last for several harrowing months. Every case of oppression is different; so is every escape.

The five escapes described in this book reflect this variety. The stories represent religious oppression on three different continents and during three different centuries. They tell about the escapes of individuals and large groups alike, of people belonging to five different faiths and subject to varying degrees of persecution. But they all share one important feature. In each case, the oppressed risked everything they had, often including their lives, for a chance to worship freely. Their stories are dramatic and inspiring.

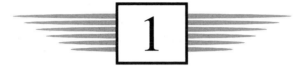

1

Roger Williams Escapes

Of all the Americans who have escaped from religious intolerance, colonial minister Roger Williams stands out. A controversial figure with decidedly unusual ideas about Christianity and the way it should be practiced, Williams enraged local religious authorities not once, but twice. Refusing to recant (give up his religious beliefs), he was shunned and oppressed for his views and activities. Both times, he was forced to escape from his oppressors in order to continue his work.

There is nothing especially odd about Williams's need to escape from persecution twice. The United States has not always been kind to members of religious minorities. Members of some American religious groups have been forced to move multiple times to find a place where they could worship as they chose. Mormons, Jews, and members of the Society of Friends, or Quakers, are just three of the American groups that have met with persecution in more than one setting.

Williams made his first escape, from England to Massachusetts, in the company of emigrants who largely shared his perspectives on Christianity and faith. Once in Massachusetts, though, his religious views changed, and his fellow emigrants now became his oppressors. As a result, Williams's second and more famous escape, from Massachusetts to the new colony of Rhode Island, was made from the people who had once supported him.

Anglicans and Puritans

At the time of Roger Williams's birth in 1603, the dominant church in England was the Anglican Church, also known as the Church of England. The Anglican Church had been founded in 1534 by King Henry VIII, and ever since then it had been known as the established, or national, church. The names referred to the tight connections between church leadership and the national government of England. So close were these connections that the king or queen of England not only served as the civil authority of the country, but was head of the Anglican Church as well.

Technically, the Church of England was Protestant; like several other denominations in northern Europe, it had broken away from Roman Catholicism during the 1500s. In reality, though, the Anglican Church included elements from both Protestant and Catholic traditions. In keeping with the standard Protestant idea that worship should be in a language accessible to the people, for instance, Anglican services were

A bishop presents the New Testament to King Henry VIII. In 1534 the king founded the Anglican Church, an institution with a close connection to England's government.

held in English rather than in Latin. But Anglican clergy, like their Catholic counterparts, formed a hierarchical system of priests, bishops, and archbishops; and the Church of England followed the Catholic model of offering ornate services that relied heavily on altars, vestments, music, and a deep sense of ceremony.

Not all the English approved of the Anglican Church. Some longed for the days when the Catholic Church had been in power. More, though, objected to church doctrines and practices from a Protestant perspective. During the late 1500s, in particular, a growing number of Anglicans argued that the Church of England had become corrupt and had lost sight of its original purpose. The dissenters soon became known as Puritans for their efforts to cleanse, or purify, the church.

While Puritans some-

Churchgoers receive communion during the 1600s. Puritans wanted to do away with such elaborate practices.

times differed in their precise complaints, they did share certain specific objections to Anglican policy. As a rule, for instance, they believed that the church was too hierarchical. Their reading of the Bible and their understanding of Christianity convinced them that congregations should choose their own ministers, with little or no interference from above. In their view, the top-heavy Anglican structure not only was unnecessary, but interfered with the relationship between humans and God.

Another objection involved the pomp and circumstance of church services. To

Puritans, the robes, incense, and musical instruments that marked a typical Church of England service were harmful distractions. In their place, Puritans championed a simpler, less showy form of worship. They believed that such a service was in keeping with biblical dictates. The plainer the worship, one early Puritan argued, the "most godly, and farthest off from superstition."[1]

"Not upon the Authority of Princes"

Probably the most important of the Puritan objections to the Church of England, though, involved the connection between the church and civil leaders. Puritans did not object to the notion that government should be influenced by religion. Nor were they hostile to the idea that there should be an established church. In medieval

Protestants and Catholics

In medieval times, there was only one acceptable form of Christianity in western and central Europe—Roman Catholicism. (Much of eastern Europe preferred Orthodox Christianity, which differed from Catholicism in several important ways.) From time to time, other variations of Christian expression cropped up within the Catholic sphere of influence, but Catholic leaders invariably crushed alternate doctrines and either killed those who held them or forced them to recant. The Catholic Church, its leaders reasoned, was a universal church; that meant its truths were clear and not subject to change or to amendment. For hundreds of years, Catholicism held a monopoly on religious thought within Western Christianity.

In the early 1500s, though, a Catholic monk named Martin Luther raised several provocative questions about Catholic doctrine. For example, he challenged the Catholic focus on doing good works to earn a place in heaven, arguing instead that only the gift of grace, freely given by God, could ensure salvation. Luther believed, too, that Catholic worship was not grounded firmly enough in the Bible. Catholics held services in the dead language of Latin and required priests to mediate between God and the congregation. The Word of God, Luther thought, ought to be at the center of worship, read to the people in a language they could understand.

Luther naively believed that the Catholic Church would prayerfully address these and other concerns he had raised. Instead, church leaders turned on him viciously. Unlike earlier dissenters, though, Luther had the support of many northern European clergy and secular leaders. He stood fast against Catholic harassment, and when it became clear that he could not reform the Catholic Church, he began a splinter church of his own. In English-speaking countries today, members of churches that hold to Luther's views are known as Protestants.

Europe, church leaders—most notably the Roman Catholic pope—had generally served as temporal, or civil, authority as well, and the Puritans were comfortable with such an arrangement.

What concerned the Puritans, instead, was the balance of church and state in sixteenth-century England. They perceived the king or queen to be primarily a civil leader, not a spiritual authority, and they disapproved of the church being ruled by someone whose ultimate loyalties might not lie with God. A leader whose main duties were temporal, the Puritans argued, should not have total control over the church. As one Puritan leader put it, church leadership needed to rest "not upon the authority of Princes, but upon the ordinance of God."[2]

Unfortunately for the Puritans, though, their ideas were met with consistent opposition from the leaders of the Anglican Church. Alarmed at the religious and political threats of Puritan theology, English rulers and church officials passed laws designed to cripple the movement. One such law, dating from the late 1500s, was aimed at those who decided to stay home rather than attend a corrupted church; it required all adults to attend Church of England services. Another law deemed it treason to deny that the English sovereign was "the only supreme governor within the realm . . . in spiritual or ecclesiastical [church-related] causes and things as [well as] temporal."[3]

Despite these measures, the movement toward Puritanism struck a chord among the English. As interest in Puritan ideas grew, the Anglican reaction became ever stronger. In 1604, King James I threatened the Puritans with serious punishment if they persisted in their complaints. "I shall make them conforme themselves [accept the Church of England as it was], or I will harrie [drive] them out of the land," James promised, "or else do worse."[4]

Still, the movement did not die. By the 1620s, despite official disapproval, Puritanism had become strong enough to make inroads into the political sphere. Early seventeenth-century Britain was governed mainly by the king—in the 1620s, James's son Charles I—but Parliament, elected in part by the people of Britain, also played a role in ruling the country. While Charles remained staunchly Anglican, many of the members of the House of Commons—the branch of government most representative of the people—were trending toward Puritanism. Open conflict seemed inevitable.

Roger Williams and the Coming Crisis

In 1628, just as the Puritan-Anglican controversy was reaching a boiling point, twenty-five-year-old Roger Williams was ordained a minister in the Church of England. Williams did not hesitate to take a side in the conflict. During his religious studies he had come to learn about Puritanism, and he found its doctrines and complaints sensible and correct.

Later that year, Williams began his ministry by serving as family chaplain in the household of a prominent English nobleman, Sir William Masham. Masham was at the center of a group of Puritan nobles who had grown disenchanted with King Charles and the Church of England. These men met frequently, sometimes at Masham's estate, to discuss religion and politics. Sometimes Williams was involved in the discussions. At every step, it seemed, he learned more about Puritan thought and doctrine. Serving as chaplain to such an important Puritan seemed the perfect position for the eager young reformer.

But soon after Williams's chaplaincy began, the fortunes of the Puritans changed considerably. On March 2, 1629, several Puritan members of the House of Commons offered a resolution condemning King Charles and his policies. The resolution insisted that the Church of England was corrupt and had strayed far from its biblical roots. "Whoever shall bring in innovation of religion," the resolution read, referring not to the proposed reforms of Puritanism but to the supposed strayings of the Anglican Church, "shall be reputed [considered] a capital enemy to this Kingdom and Commonwealth."[5]

A fierce and angry debate ensued, during which supporters of the resolution actually held the anti-Puritan Speaker of the House in his chair to prevent him from stopping the proceedings altogether. Although the resolution passed, the Puritan victory did not last. Furious, Charles used the full extent of his powers to crack down on those who had defied him. He arrested the authors of the resolution. Then, Charles dissolved Parliament altogether. The decision, he announced in a slap at Puritan thinkers, was to uphold "the true religion and doctrine established in the Church of England."[6]

Flight to Massachusetts

Charles's angry response ushered in a new era in the oppression of the Puritans. The new bishop of London, William Laud, seemed to take pleasure in persecuting those who continued to speak out against the policies and actions of the Church of England. In addition to levying fines and sending Puritans to prison, Laud's men tortured those who spoke up for Puritanism. The bishop was particularly eager to silence Puritan-leaning priests, whom he called "the most dangerous enemies of the state. . . . They awakened the people's dissatisfaction, and therefore must be suppressed."[7]

Laud may or may not have been thinking specifically of Roger Williams when he wrote those words. Certainly Williams was among the more enthusiastic of English Puritans in his condemnation of Anglican policies. Despite the personal dangers of opposing the established church, he wrote essays countering Laud's arguments against Puritan reform. In general, throughout 1629 and much of 1630, Williams kept up a steady barrage of complaints against the Anglican leadership.

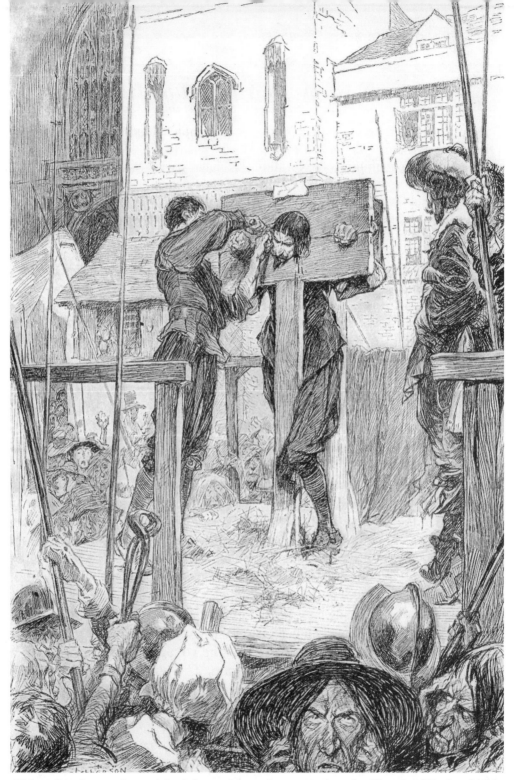

Bishop Laud severely punished those who spoke out against the Church of England. This Puritan's ears are cut off because he wrote a book that attacked the Anglican Church.

God's Nostrils and *The Bloody Tenet*

Even when common sense demanded it, Roger Williams was never one to keep his opinions to himself. Nor did he find it easy to modify his phrasings and rhetorical flourishes to suit the sensibilities of those who read or heard him. As much as any matter of doctrine, this headstrong behavior landed him in trouble with the authorities in both England and in Massachusetts. Nevertheless, it cannot be denied that Williams had a way with words. His images were bold and direct, and his meaning was always clear. Compulsory attendance at Sunday services, for instance, Williams declared, was "forced worship"—and "forced worship," he argued, as quoted in William G. McLoughlin's *Rhode Island*, "stinks in God's nostrils."

Similarly, when Williams wrote a book urging religious tolerance, he entitled it *The Bloody Tenet. Tenet* means "belief"; the blood, Williams argued, was from the people murdered because their beliefs did not match those of the majority. Massachusetts minister John Cotton, who believed in an established Puritan church, quickly responded with a pro-persecution book of his own, which he rather gently called *The Bloody Tenet Washed and Made White*. To this, Williams replied once more, this time with a book entitled *The Bloody Tenet Made Yet More Bloody by Mr. Cotton's Endeavor to Wash It White in the Blood of the Lamb.*

Whether Laud had Williams in mind or not, there is no doubt that Williams came under the intense scrutiny of Laud and his assistants in 1630. It seemed clear that Williams would be arrested, jailed, and tortured if he did not act quickly. Many of Williams's friends and fellow Puritan agitators had already fled England. Most had headed for Massachusetts Bay, a British colony just being established in North America.

Williams decided to join his friends in the New World. In the fall of 1630, he hurried from his home just ahead of Bishop Laud's men. He and his wife, Mary, sped to the seaport of Bristol, where they boarded a ship bound for North America. Williams was in such a rush that he did not say good-bye to some of his oldest friends. "It was bitter as death to me," he wrote the daughter of one of these men, "when Bishop Laud pursued me out of this land . . . [and I dared] not acquaint [your father] with my conscience and my flight."[8]

The voyage to Massachusetts was grim. The ship left Bristol on December 1, 1630, and did not arrive in Boston until February 5, more than two months later. Roger Williams would never again live in England. For better or for worse, he had escaped Bishop Laud and would now settle in America.

A Puritan Colony

To most Puritans of the time, Massachusetts seemed a dream come true. In isolated New England, they anticipated being able to worship as they chose. In theory, they were still subject to England's laws and bound to follow the rules of the Anglican Church. In practice, though, three thousand miles of ocean separated them from King Charles. As a result, the churches of Massachusetts used a distinctively Puritan form of worship.

Better yet, each British colony was expected to be largely self-governing. Seizing this opportunity, the Puritans of Massachusetts had structured their colonial government along Puritan lines. In particular, they had established separate civil and religious authorities. A government, led by a Puritan lawyer named John Winthrop, made and enforced the laws. The largest share of the power, however, was vested not in Winthrop and his fellow magistrates, but instead in the ministers of the colony.

A group of Puritans worships in a small church in Massachusetts. Puritans worshipped as they chose even though they were still tied to the Church of England.

In fact, much of the reason for the Massachusetts civil government was to enforce the dictates of the church. In the new colony, just as in England, there were fines for refusing to attend services, and all citizens paid taxes to support the church. In New England, though, the established church was not ornate and Anglican, but simple and Puritan. Most of the New England colonial regulations, likewise, reflected Puritan notions of proper behavior. In accordance with Puritan ideas, for instance, Massachusetts residents—whether Puritan or not—were prohibited from carrying out most nonreligious activities on Sunday.

Although the churches of Massachusetts were Puritan in both worship and structure, the leaders of the new colony were not willing to reject Anglicanism altogether. They made it clear that they still considered themselves members of the Church of England. Church leaders took this position in part for political reasons—it was wise not to offend the authorities in England, after all—but mostly because it matched their understanding of theology. The problem was not the established church, but the way in which the church ran its business.

Not all Puritans, however, agreed with the ministers of Massachusetts on this matter. Another group, called the Separatists, believed that there was nothing godly about the doctrines and policies of the Anglican Church. While the Massachusetts ministers had chosen to purify the church from within, the Separatists had decided to abandon it. As their name suggests, they strove to leave the Church of England to set up their own faith community. Like the non-Separatist Puritans, though, they had generally met with failure; the Anglican Church resisted their efforts to secede.

Although they agreed on many matters of faith and doctrine, Separatists and non-Separatist Puritans had frequently been at odds over their different strategies. But the distinctions between the two groups loomed particularly large in Massachusetts. The Pilgrims, a group of Separatist Puritans, had settled in nearby Plymouth in 1620—several years before the Massachusetts Bay group arrived. The two groups were neighbors, but they viewed one another with suspicion and distaste.

Williams in Massachusetts Bay Colony

Roger Williams received a warm welcome when he and Mary arrived in Massachusetts in 1631. He was personally acquainted with many of the new colony's leaders, both secular and religious. They knew him as bright, enthusiastic, and determined; Winthrop, the colonial governor, noted approvingly in his diary that Williams was a "godly minister."[9] Before long, Williams had received his first call, or job offer to serve as a minister, at a church in Boston. It seemed to Winthrop and the other colonial officials that young Williams would fit perfectly into Massachusetts life.

Massachusetts Bay colonists welcome Roger Williams. Williams quickly left the colony, however, when he realized he did not share the colonists' non-Separatist views.

They were disappointed and surprised, then, when Williams turned down the position he had been offered. Although everyone believed Williams to have been a non-Separatist while in England, he had changed his opinion upon coming to the New World. The churchgoers of Boston, he noted, were determined to maintain their ties with the Church of England, and that decision was unacceptable to him. In his view, the entire Massachusetts structure of government was deeply flawed. As he saw it, civil law should have nothing at all to do with the religious establishment. In short, it was not the business of the state to enforce the rules of the church.

This was not a particularly Separatist position. It seems to have sprung from Williams's own conscience and his interpretation of the Bible. Taken to its logical conclusion, Williams's views would make it impossible to have religious laws. It would be impossible to have an established church at all.

To the ministers and governors of the Massachusetts Bay Colony, Williams's position seemed extremely dangerous. Williams's support of a separated church and state suggested nothing less than complete religious liberty, and they had no interest in that concept. Their quarrel with Anglicanism had not been that it was an established church, but merely that it was not structured the way they wished. To them, the solution was to establish a new and better church, not to rid the land of established churches—those officially approved by the state—altogether.

Williams was soon offered a position at a church in Salem, just north of Boston. The congregation there had a tendency toward Separatist thought, and the people of Salem were intrigued by the radical ideas Williams expressed. But the ministers of Massachusetts intervened. In a letter, they sharply urged the Salem congregation to rescind their offer. The Salem church gave in. Roger Williams had been blackballed.

More Troubles

Williams quickly left the Massachusetts Bay Colony to serve at a Separatist church in Plymouth. Williams enjoyed much of his time in Plymouth. In addition to his ministerial duties, Williams got to know some of the region's Native Americans. He learned words and phrases in Indian languages, and he grew to respect native culture and ideas. As he wrote in a poem directed at less tolerant colonists, "Boast not, proud English, of thy birth and blood. / Thy brother Indian is by birth as good."[10]

But in fact, he was little better accepted in Plymouth than he had been in Boston. While the Separatists admired Williams's refusal to accept the Church of England, they were no readier than the ministers of Massachusetts to approve his doctrines of religious liberty. The people of Plymouth also resented Williams's insistence on the rights and fundamental equality of the Native Americans. All in all, wrote Plymouth governor William Bradford, Williams was "very unsettled in judgment."[11] By the fall of 1633, Williams had worn out his welcome in Plymouth.

Fortunately for Williams, he had a place to go. The church at Salem had invited him again, this time in an unofficial capacity—in part to avoid offending the leaders of the Massachusetts colony. In this position, though, Williams agitated more loudly than before. He preached regularly about the corrupt Church of England, the need for religious freedom, and the rights of the Indians.

Salem appreciated his words, but the rest of Massachusetts did not. The more he spoke, the more frustrated the leaders of the colony grew. Late in 1635, a council of magistrates and clergy determined that Williams had espoused "new and dangerous opinions against the authority of the magistrates."[12] As a penalty, they agreed, he would be banished from the colony.

Williams had expected the verdict and had already made plans for his next step. Together with some of his Salem followers, he intended to move to a remote area of the colony to found a more

Anne Hutchinson

Roger Williams was not the only person forced to flee from the Massachusetts Bay Colony. Not long after Williams's escape, a Puritan woman named Anne Hutchinson began stirring up trouble within the New England church. Hutchinson—devout, intelligent, and the mother of fourteen children—began interpreting the Bible for herself and sharing her thoughts with others, even when her opinions conflicted with those of the ministers.

Hutchinson's right to interpret the Bible for herself, at least in theory, was approved by standard Puritan doctrine. But she was acting in opposition to the wishes of the ministers, and the threat she represented to the established church seemed greater than the risks of not following Puritan theory. Hutchinson was censured, tried, and banned from the colony. She eventually made her way to

Williams's Rhode Island. Later on, she moved to New York, where she was killed by Native Americans. The leaders of Massachusetts unanimously saw her murder as an act of divine judgment.

Anne Hutchinson defends herself during her trial before Massachusetts Bay authorities.

tolerant church. But the Massachusetts authorities refused to permit the move. Deciding to get rid of him completely, they sent a ship to Salem to return him to England.

A Second Escape

If Massachusetts would not have Williams, it was certain that England would not want him either. Williams knew that King Charles and the bishops would likely arrest him as soon as he arrived; there was a good chance he would never again be a free man. In January 1636, just before the ship was due to arrive in Salem, Williams made the only move still available to him: He fled from Salem in search of a place of

Williams prepares to flee Salem after learning that Massachusetts leaders planned to send him back to England.

refuge. As Williams put it many years afterward, he had been "unkindly and unchristianly . . . driven from [his] house and land and wife and children in the midst of a New England winter."[13]

Although Williams wrote voluminously about his work and thoughts, he never described his escape from Massachusetts in much detail. Consequently, some questions about the journey will never be fully resolved. Still, Williams's own recollections do reveal some information about his route and experiences. So do the writings of those who knew him. Together, the available

source material gives a good indication of what Williams's second escape might have been like.

It is certain that Williams did not travel alone. "I gave leave to W. Harris, then poor and destitute, to come along in my Company,"[14] he wrote in a letter years later; the letter went on to name three others who had accompanied him on the trip. (Some sources suggest there was a fifth follower as well, not mentioned in this letter.) Most of his companions seem to have been impoverished young men, on the fringes of Puritan society and perhaps most likely to respond to a radical message of religious change. Certainly all were ardent followers of Williams, and all lived in or around Salem.

It is also clear that the conditions of the escape were extremely difficult. As Williams indicated, the journey took place in the dead of winter. Heavy snow covered the ground, slowing Williams and his companions and forcing them to struggle through high drifts. Because it was wintertime, too, finding shelter was an absolute necessity. It was simply not feasible to sleep out in the open, as it would have been in August or even in May.

Finally, it is known that Williams received help from the local Native Americans. "If the Indians which were the natives of the land had not [helped] him," wrote a colonial historian, "hee might have sufered deth, but they was very kind to him and [helped] him a long in his [journey]."[15] For two reasons, that help is not surprising. First, the Native Americans knew all about survival in a New England winter, while the travelers, as relative newcomers to North America, did not. Second, Williams had been a friend to the Indians of southeastern Massachusetts. If he was in need, there was every reason to believe that they would help him.

Rhode Island

In all, Williams later claimed, the journey took fourteen weeks. During at least some of this time, it is reasonable to suppose that the men stayed with the Indians, probably those of the Narragansett or Wampanoag tribes.

During the rest, however, the men presumably wandered throughout present-day southeastern Massachusetts. Their precise route will never be known.

In the early spring of 1636, however, Williams and his companions found themselves on the banks of the Seekonk River near what is now the town of Rehoboth, Massachusetts. Here, Williams believed, he had come far enough from the colony's civil and religious authorities that they would not try to pursue him. Indeed, he thought he was outside the boundaries of the colony altogether. Williams negotiated with the local Indians for a plot of land; then he sent one of his companions back to Salem with the information that his escape had been successful.

Williams was indeed outside the borders of the Massachusetts Bay Colony—but he was not quite beyond the land claimed by the Plymouth Separatists. Receiving a friendly letter to that effect from the governor of Plymouth, Williams decided to move on once again. But this move was different from the others—he was not making an escape. And this time, his move would be permanent.

Later that spring, Williams headed across the Seekonk and came to the Moshassuck River. The local Native Americans offered him a section of land in what is now eastern Rhode Island, and Williams quickly accepted. His search was over. Twice he had escaped from persecution. At last, he had found a place where he could worship

Native Americans welcome Williams upon his arrival to Rhode Island. He and others established the colony of Rhode Island as one that tolerated all religions.

as he chose, free from the interference of those who had scorned his ideas and tried to force him to recant.

Williams sent for his wife, children, and supporters and set to work building the city of Providence in the new colony of Rhode Island. The colony would be founded in part on the principle of religious liberty; it would welcome members of all faiths. As Williams put it years later, "I desired [that the colony] might be a shelter for persons distressed of conscience."[16] His own years of suffering from persecution had given him a deep understanding and sympathy for other victims of religious oppression.

2

Escape from Srebrenica

ONE OF THE saddest chapters in the history of religious intolerance took place during the summer of 1995 in Srebrenica (pronounced sre-bre-NEET-sa), a small city in the Bosnian region of Yugoslavia. During a four-day period that July, after several years of bitter fighting between Christian and Muslim groups in Bosnia, Christian troops from nearby towns slaughtered thousands of Srebrenica's Muslims. At least seven thousand Muslims were killed in a succession of massacres, marking Europe's worst violence since the end of World War II.

The hostility directed at the city's Muslim population was widespread and ferocious. Nevertheless, many Muslims managed to avoid the mass executions. Before the massacre took place, and in some cases while it was going on, these people fled the city and successfully reached safe zones elsewhere in Yugoslavia.

Serbs, Croats, and Muslims

The southeastern European nation of Yugoslavia came into being in the early twentieth century. The nation brought together several different countries, each with its own culture, language, and religious expression. The two most populous groups within the nation were Serbs and Croats, most of whom lived, respectively, in the Yugoslav republics of Serbia and Croatia. However, Yugoslavia was also home to Slovenians, Montenegrins, Albanians, and many other ethnic groups.

Although the country as a whole was multiethnic, the individual regions that made up Yugoslavia were less so. Five of the country's six states, or republics, had decided majorities of one group or another. The exception was the central Yugoslav state of Bosnia and Herzegovina, usually called simply Bosnia. By 1990, Bosnia had about 4.5 million people, about 30 percent of them Serb and another 20 percent Croat. Most of the rest—approximately 45 percent of the total—were Muslim.

The three groups were similar in some significant ways. They spoke the same language, Serbo-Croatian, and they came from the same racial stock. Socially and culturally, the three groups had much in common. There was only one significant way in which these groups were different: their religions. The Serbs were Orthodox Christians, while the Croats were Roman Catholic, and the Muslims were not Christian at all.

But under the charismatic Communist leader Marshal Josip Broz Tito, who ruled Yugoslavia after World War II, the religious differences seemed unimportant. Tito discouraged expressions of nationalist feeling and played

President Marshal Tito addresses the Yugoslav congress at his inauguration in 1953. Tito encouraged religious and ethnic tolerance during his time in office.

down religious and ethnic differences, so in Bosnia, in particular, tolerance prevailed. Friendships between people of different faiths were common. "We used to play football together," recalled one Muslim man about his boyhood Serb friends. "We used to go out at night, and if we didn't go out, we used to spend the evenings together on our street."[17] Even weddings were often multiethnic; a quarter of all Bosnian marriages matched couples of different religions.

Religion and History

The tolerance, however, masked a long history of religious tension among the three groups—particularly the Serbs and the Muslims. During medieval times, the entire area had been Christian. But in the fourteenth century, the Muslim Ottoman Empire, based in present-day Turkey, invaded much of southeastern Europe. At the Battle of Kosovo, another state in Yugoslavia, Christian soldiers were soundly defeated by the attackers. The Muslims quickly asserted their control over most of the region—an area that included Bosnia as well as Serbia, the ancestral homeland of the Serbs.

Now under Muslim dominance, the defeated Christians were faced with a dilemma: whether to convert to Islam or to keep their Christian faith. The Ottoman conquerors clearly favored their Muslim subjects, and for this reason many Bosnians decided to convert. These, for the most part, are the ancestors of the present-day Bosnian Muslims. Others decided to maintain their identity as Christians; their descendants are the Serbs and Croats of today.

For generations, the descendants of these Christians chafed under Ottoman rule. That was particularly true of the Serbs, whose country remained largely in the hands of the Turks for nearly five hundred years. Not until the nineteenth century did Christian groups manage to drive the Ottomans back toward Turkey and reclaim control of their former territory. Still, by the middle of the twentieth century the differences and hostilities between Bosnian Muslims and Christians seemed forgotten. The question was whether the new harmony had replaced the old hostilities forever—or whether religious intolerance would once again make an appearance.

Nationalism and Violence

The answer came soon after the death of Marshal Tito in 1980. It quickly became evident that Tito had not eliminated nationalist sentiment; he had simply held it in check through the force of his personality. During his reign, people had identified themselves not so much as Serbs, Croats, or Slovenians, but as Yugoslavs. But now, as the country's new leaders began moving toward a more democratic form of government, the situation reversed itself. The republics began to view one another with doubt and outright suspicion. A wave of nationalism surged through much of Yugoslavia.

Slobodan Milosevic asserts in a 1989 speech that Muslims must be driven out of Serb areas.

The Serbs, in particular, seemed caught up in nationalist feeling. In 1989, for instance, Serb official Slobodan Milosevic commemorated the Battle of Kosovo with a speech that seemed to carry veiled threats against other Yugoslav republics and peoples. "Six centuries [after Kosovo]," he said, "we are again engaged in conflicts and disputes. These aren't yet armed battles, but such things can't be ruled out."[18] Milosevic's words seemed to promise a resurgence of Serbia at the expense of the rest of the nation.

As nationalism increased, tensions worsened even in multiethnic Bosnia. In 1990, the newly democratic republic held its first-ever free elections. Three major parties formed, each one established along ethnic and religious lines. Because Muslims held the greatest share of voters, the Muslim party won the most seats in the legislature. The outcome disappointed and angered thousands of Bosnian Serbs and Croats. They feared that the Muslims, once in power, would try to oppress them just as the Muslims' ancestors had done centuries before.

War Comes to Bosnia

Soon after the 1990 elections, the six republics that composed Yugoslavia began to fall apart. In 1991, the republics of Slovenia and Croatia decided to secede. The following year, Bosnian Muslims and Croats voted overwhelmingly to secede as well. Bosnian Serbs, however, boycotted the election and refused to abide by the results. With support from Milosevic and the people of Serbia, they began driving Muslims from heavily Serb areas of Bosnia, intending to join these parts of the country to Serbia itself. The Muslims could not match the Serb armies or firepow-

er. By 1995, millions of non-Serbs—most of them Muslims—had been chased from their homes, and the Serbs controlled over 70 percent of Bosnian territory. War had come to Bosnia.

As the war progressed, Serb soldiers grew increasingly vicious in their treatment of Bosnia's Muslims. Some were beaten by troops before being expelled from their homes. Thousands of women were brutally raped, sometimes by a dozen soldiers in succession. And prison camps reminiscent of the Nazi

Religious Persecution Grows in Bosnia

With the coming of the Bosnian war, the tolerance that had marked relations between the religious groups of the republic disappeared. Many Muslims spoke bitterly about Serbs who had once been their friends, but who now participated in their oppression. Indeed, Serbs confiscated Bosnian property and forced their Muslim neighbors onto transports bound for Muslim-majority areas of Bosnia. Serb soldiers bombed Muslim mosques; Serb officials closed Islamic schools. In some cases, Bosnian Croats took the opportunity to harass Muslims as well. The question of religious affiliation became paramount in Bosnia. Those who were Muslim were increasingly persecuted for their faith—and for the political beliefs that stemmed from their religious identity.

Serbs and Croats quickly began to suspect the worst of their Muslim neighbors. Rumors spread that Muslim doctors rou-

tinely castrated male Christian newborns and sterilized every Christian woman they treated. Many Serbs and Croats became convinced that the Bosnian Muslims were in league with repressive, intolerant Middle Eastern nations. As the political leader of Bosnia's Croats put it, as quoted in Phillip Corwin's *Dubious Mandate*, "The [Bosnian] Muslims want to establish an Islamic fundamentalist state. . . . Catholics and Orthodox [Christians] alike will be eradicated."

In fact, none of this was true. The Muslim edge in numbers came not from medical atrocities, but from a relatively high birthrate. And while there were some ties between the Muslims of the Middle East and the Muslims of Bosnia, there is no evidence that Bosnian Muslims had any interest in establishing a purely Islamic state. For the most part, they were willing, indeed eager, to continue living in a pluralistic republic.

Three men carry a victim of a 1994 bombing in Bosnia. Such attacks by Serbs against Muslims were common.

era were built for the purpose of torturing captured Muslims. "One guard," reported journalist Greg Campbell, "would nonchalantly ask a captive which of his eyes . . . he liked best. The loser was gouged out."[19]

Despite the violence, the Serb soldiers were not at first able to remove all traces of Islam from the area they claimed as their own. Under the protection of the United Nations and other international organizations, several heavily Muslim towns and cities in those regions had been declared "safe zones" for Muslims. The Serbs resented the establishment of these safe zones, but initially had little choice but to respect their boundaries.

The first of the safe zones established by the United Nations was the eastern Bosnian town of Srebrenica. Muslims made up about three-quarters of the city's prewar population of about thirty-seven thousand; the remainder were Serbs. But in the first days of fighting, the composition of the population had changed considerably. The outnumbered Serbs had left the area, while Muslims from other districts sought refuge in the town. By March 1993, when the safe zone was declared, sixty thousand Muslims were crammed into thirty square miles of territory.

The United Nations tried to keep the Serbs at bay by sending a few thousand peacekeeping soldiers into Srebrenica to protect the Muslims and to ensure that the Serbs observed the safe zone. But the peacekeepers were lacking in weapons, supplies, and, most of all, unqualified support from UN military leaders. In July 1995, Serb armies seized their opportunity and attacked Srebrenica. Even with the help of a few thousand Muslim soldiers in the town, the peacekeepers could not hold back the onrushing Serbs. Within a few hours, Srebrenica had fallen.

Making for Tuzla

As they moved deeper into the city, the Serb commanders called upon the Muslim fighters to surrender. Those men who gave themselves up, Serb leaders promised, would be treated fairly and with respect. But few of the Muslim soldiers believed the promise. They had heard too many stories of Serb wartime atrocities to believe that surrendering would mean anything but death.

Instead, between ten and fifteen thousand Muslim soldiers and other men of fighting age decided to escape to either Tuzla or Zepa, Bosnian cities still held by Muslim forces. Tuzla was a forty-mile journey through Serb-held territory; Zepa was closer but as isolated as Srebrenica. Still, most Srebrenican men believed that they had no choice but to go. "We're going to have to run for it," one man recalled telling a friend. "This town is going to fall, and the people here are all done for."[20]

If the need arose, these soldiers were willing to charge the Serb army and fight their way through. To their surprise, however, the troops at the front of the Serb columns (army) allowed the Muslims to pass through their ranks, on the understanding that they head directly for Tuzla. At first the Muslim soldiers were relieved by the gesture. But as they passed by the Serb soldiers, they began to wonder if they were walking into a trap.

They were right to be concerned. The maneuver had forced the Muslim men into a column five miles long and just yards wide—an arrangement vulnerable to attack. Worse, the men were highly visible as they made their way across the Bosnian countryside. And most of them no longer carried working weapons. Under these circumstances, ambushing them would be easy.

The group left in late morning. The day was hot, and the trail was rugged; by evening the men had advanced only about four miles. All along the way, Serbs had occasionally fired on them, killing several and terrifying those who remained. As night fell, the group stopped to rest in a forest. Then, all at once, the woods around them seemed to explode. Serb soldiers riddled the Muslims with gunfire, grenades, and shells from an antiaircraft gun hidden in a nearby clearing.

The ambush probably killed no more than 125. But whatever confidence the Muslims had once had was now gone. Except for one large group of about 4,000 men toward the front of the column, the Muslims fled singly and in small groups into the wilderness. Around them, on all sides, were Serb soldiers. There was no going back to Srebrenica, but it looked as if there was no going forward, either.

A woman runs through an area of Sarajevo, Bosnia's captial, where Serb snipers shot Muslim civilians on a daily basis.

Srebrenica and the Siege

Conditions in Srebrenica changed dramatically during the war. Once, the townspeople had enjoyed a high standard of living, with most residents able to afford goods like cars and VCRs. By the time the city had been declared a safe zone, though, many of these modern conveniences were gone. The electricity had been shut off throughout the town, and residents were forced to break up furniture to burn for fuel.

Over the next two years, the situation worsened. Medical care became almost nonexistent, and disease ran rampant in the crowded, unsanitary city. Visitors found the stench appalling, especially in the summer. Worse yet, food became more and more scarce. The small section of countryside within the safe area could not produce nearly enough food for all Srebrenica's citizens and refugees.

Western nations and fellow Bosnian Muslims did their best to alleviate these conditions. They frequently shipped food and medicine to the city. According to international convention, the Serbs were supposed to allow these supplies to reach Srebrenica. Instead, though, the Serb soldiers who surrounded the city prevented most of these goods from reaching their destination. The effect was similar to that of a medieval siege, during which one army would surround another and prevent people and goods from moving in and out. If the siege was successful, the defending army would eventually surrender—or starve.

Through the Woods

Most of the men pressed on, hoping to find a path between the Serb army units. But over the next few days, their trek became a nightmare. The barrage of gunfire did not stop. The men dodged shells and bullets as they made their way toward Tuzla and Zepa. Food became scarce and sometimes nonexistent. Streams filled with human waste; fresh water was hard to find. Even sleep was risky. Serb troops roamed through fields at night, killing all the sleeping Muslims they could find.

The constant attacks shattered nerves as well as bodies. "Some people in the group began to hallucinate," recalled Ilijas Pilav. "They shouted and screamed and betray[ed] our position. . . . Some armed men completely panicked and opened fire randomly. They shot a few of their own men. We had to overpower them with force."[21] Even those who maintained their grip on reality found the mental stress almost unbearable.

Over the next few days, the Serbs mercilessly picked off the Muslims as they made their way toward safety. Many of the Muslim soldiers, despairing of ever reaching their goal, gave themselves up rather than spend another night of uncertainty in the forests. Thousands more were captured, and many others were killed. Most who were seriously wounded died of their injuries; the Muslims could offer each other little first aid, and there was no help available in the nearby Serb-controlled towns and villages.

"I Ate Only Apples"

Still, some men continued their struggle to escape. Reasonably well-armed and able to stay together, they managed to fight their way toward Tuzla. At one point, they took a Serb officer hostage and used him as a bargaining chip to advance a few miles toward their goal.

Closer to Muslim-controlled territory, they captured a Serb tank and turned it against their enemies. After hours of bitter fighting, the Serb line outside the Muslim-controlled area near Tuzla finally gave way. A week after leaving Srebrenica, about thirty-five hundred survivors of the battle struggled into central Bosnia.

They were not the only ones. In the days and weeks to come, hundreds more men slipped across the boundary, alone and in small groups. Many of these men had suffered terribly on their way to safety. Without effective weapons, they were unable to shoot their way to freedom or to capture enemy hostages; instead, they had been forced to rely on their wits. Often this meant hiding in dense forests for days at a time. Members of one group spent nearly two weeks concealed in a thicket while waiting for Serb troops to withdraw from the area. "I ate only apples for seven days,"[22] one of the men recalled afterward.

These smaller groups suffered in other ways, too. For safety reasons, most traveled at night, when it was almost impossible to see the trail. Unfamiliar with the countryside, they were never sure if they were traveling in the right direction. Even their clothing worked against them; their military outfits marked them as escaping soldiers, making them inviting targets for Serb troops and sympathizers. Under such circumstances, it was astonishing that so many Muslim soldiers reached safety.

Their escapes, though, came at a terrible cost. Many of these survivors had been wounded. Most had eaten virtually nothing throughout their trek. Their shoes had fallen apart; their feet were bloody; all were in desperate need of sleep. Still, they had escaped death and capture. They had reached the safety of the Muslim lines.

Massacre

The Muslim soldiers had predicted that they would be killed if they surrendered or were captured, and many civilians in Srebrenica believed the same. As the Serb troops moved in on July 11, 1995, thousands of unarmed civilian Muslims streamed out of their homes, hurrying to avoid Serb bullets. "Everywhere was luggage, dumped to run faster,"[23] recalled one observer. Most of the refugees hurried toward the Dutch compound just outside the city limits, but the compound was too small to offer safety to all those trying to escape. The Muslims of Srebrenica were prisoners at the mercy of their attackers.

Unidentified victims of the Srebrenica massacre lay in rows of body bags. An estimated seven thousand Muslims were killed in the area in July 1995.

At first, as they had done with the Muslim soldiers, the Serbs made promises designed to calm their worried captives. "There is no need to be frightened," Serb general Ratko Mladic assured the Muslims. "You'll be taken to a safe place."[24] His troops encouraged the refugees to board buses bound for areas of Bosnia still held by the Muslims. Hearing these promises, some of the Srebrenica Muslims began to relax.

But the assurances were lies. Although some women, children, and elderly men were indeed shipped to Tuzla, more were sent to Turkey and other nations, where they were housed in squalid refugee camps. Many of the women were raped. The younger Muslim men were quickly separated from their families by Serb troops. Some were informed that they would be led to safety by an alternate route. Others were told that they were needed for questioning.

Over the next few days, these Muslim men were taken to warehouses, athletic fields, and the streets and alleys of Srebrenica itself. There they were joined by many of the Muslim soldiers who had surrendered or been captured on their way to Tuzla. The men were herded into corners or told to line up. Then, in mass executions reminiscent of the Nazi era, they were murdered.

Escape from the Massacres

For most of the victims of the massacre, escape was impossible. They were watched by men with automatic weapons, and they were in no physical condition to resist. Moreover, Serb actions and statements lulled most Muslims into thinking themselves safer than they actually were. "We will give you some food [and] move you to a cooler place,"[25] Mladic assured one group of prisoners an hour before they were killed. For many Muslims, the first indication of the Serbs' true plans came only when the firing began.

The Serbs were thorough. Most of the victims were shot more than once. Serb marksmen searched through the dead for possible survivors. "Put a bullet through all the heads," ordered one army commander, "even if they're cold."[26] In most cases, the soldiers obeyed. Under these circumstances, the odds of escaping the warehouses and gyms were slim indeed.

Still, an occasional Muslim survived the massacres. A few were wounded by the gunfire, but not killed. Others were never struck by a bullet. These men dived to the floor when the shooting started so as not to attract the attention of the Serb troops. Hakija Husejnovic, for example, burrowed under a pile of dead bodies for further safety. He kept his head down and remained absolutely motionless for twenty-four hours, until he was sure his captors had gone.

Of course, surviving the gunfire did not guarantee escape. Those who did not die were nevertheless mentally and physically traumatized. Hit by four bullets but still alive, Nezad Avdic considered asking a Serb to kill him so his ordeal would be over. Avdic, Husejnovic, and others in similar positions were stranded in territory newly captured by the Serbs. If they were recaptured, they would surely be added to another group of men doomed to execution.

Still, a surprising number of those who survived did escape to safety. Avdic and another survivor of the same massacre joined forces and headed through the forests together, eventually arriving in central Bosnia without being captured by the Serbs. Husejnovic scurried through a hole in the side of the warehouse and hid briefly in a cornfield, then made his way to Zepa. Both men later provided valuable information to international authorities trying to determine what had happened at Srebrenica.

Mevludin Oric and Hurem Suljic

Probably the most dramatic escape from the killing fields was the flight of

Mevludin Oric and Hurem Suljic. Oric was a young soldier who had been captured while trying to reach Tuzla. Suljic, in contrast, was a retired carpenter, a man in his fifties with a bad leg. Until the evening of July 14, the two had never met.

That day, though, both men were among hundreds of prisoners transported to a field thirty miles from Srebrenica. After arriving at the field in buses, the men were told to line up in small groups. Then they were machine-gunned. Virtually all were killed on the spot. Through pure luck, however, both Oric and Suljic avoided being struck by a bullet when their turns came. Both men played dead, while around them the shooting continued.

Throughout the day and into the evening, the Serbs kept up the firing. Men fell almost as quickly as they could be dragged off the buses, and corpses covered the grass. When it got dark, the Serbs turned on the lights of a nearby bulldozer so they could see what they were doing. Soldiers paced through the field, shooting again at those who moved, but through it all Suljic and Oric attracted no attention.

Oric's strategy was to stay perfectly still, which he did despite being badly bitten by ants—and despite the fact that a Serb soldier actually stepped on him while killing one of Oric's cousins. Suljic, however, used a different tactic. He had fallen in the center of the

The remains of two bodies and pieces of clothing lie on the soil above a mass grave site in Srebrenica.

field and worried that he could not escape detection in such an exposed place. Taking an enormous risk, he waited till the soldiers' backs were turned. Then he wriggled into a nearby thicket. The bushes could not conceal him perfectly, but Suljic believed they would be better than nothing. Then he, like Oric, waited until the carnage ended.

Near midnight, the Serbs finished for the day. They shut off the bulldozer's lights and left the field by truck, planning to come back later to bury the evidence of the massacre. About ten minutes after they left, Oric stood up. The moment he did so, however, he heard a voice from about ten yards away. Terrified, Oric turned to run; then he realized the voice belonged to another prisoner. It was Suljic.

There seemed to be no Serbs left on the field, but the two men hurried to escape before the enemy could return. Oric led the way uphill into the forest, with Suljic slowly stumbling along behind; every step was painful because he had lost the orthopedic shoe that made walking manageable for him. As they reached the edge of the woods, a truck carrying Serb soldiers returned to the field. Panicking, the two disappeared into the forest before the truck pulled to a halt. They had not been seen.

The two men slept fitfully in the forest that night. They knew they would be easy targets for Serb troops if they tried to travel far, and both believed

Casting Blame

While it was certainly true that the Muslims suffered the most during the war, local Serbs in heavily Muslim areas of Bosnia had been persecuted before the war. As the conflict got under way, Muslims committed their share of wartime atrocities. Vistors to the area often came away with the belief that the leaders of both sides, as United Nations political officer Phillip Corwin put it in his book *Dubious Mandate*, "were merely gangsters wearing coats and ties."

Not all observers were quick to embrace the widely held view that the Serbs were worse than the Muslims. Corwin, among others, believed that the Bosnian Serbs had valid complaints about the way they were being treated. Others argued that if the size of the armies and the power of the weapons had been reversed, the Serbs would have suffered just as badly as the Muslims.

The historical record, however, is clear. The Muslims of Bosnia suffered a good deal more than did the Serbs or even the Croats, and they were the only victims of major genocidal attacks such as the one at Srebrenica. There was no shortage of religious oppression in 1990s Bosnia, but it was much worse when it was aimed at the Muslims.

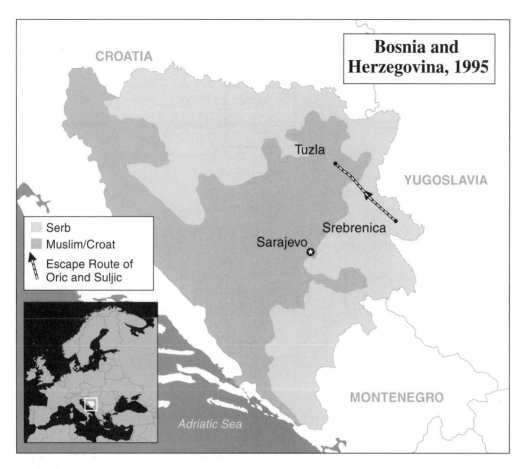

Bosnia and Herzegovina, 1995

CROATIA

Tuzla

YUGOSLAVIA

Srebrenica

Sarajevo

Serb
Muslim/Croat
Escape Route of
Oric and Suljic

MONTENEGRO

Adriatic Sea

their chances of success were slim. The next morning, however, the men spotted a river that they knew was near Muslim-held territory. The knowledge gave them hope and courage, but it did not provide them with a way across the heavily guarded frontier. Machine guns lined the border, and the two men believed that the Serbs had booby-trapped the stream that marked the boundary. They tried to cross the border at a remote location, but were driven back by gunfire.

Despite having little or no food and scarcely any access to water, Suljic and Oric did not give in. By this time they had met up with two other survivors of the massacres. On the morning of July 19, the four men decided to split up for safety. Oric headed up a steep hill, while the others tried paths that led in other directions.

They had made the right move. By that afternoon, Oric, Suljic, and both of their companions had found a way across the border and were safely in Muslim territory. The journey had been long and terrifying, but they had reached a place of refuge. Against all odds, they had escaped the horrors of Srebrenica.

3

Leaving the Soviet Union

SOMETIMES, PEOPLE ESCAPE from oppression in dramatic fashion. Outsmarting prison guards and secret-police officers, they scurry unseen into forests or mountains near their homes. There they hide in caves or dense thickets, evading detection until it is safe to move on. With the help of sympathetic people in the area, they eventually make their way by night to international borders, which they cross by swimming across rivers or, perhaps, digging tunnels. Only then, after a series of dangerous and compelling events, are they free.

Not all escapes, however, follow this pattern. Some escapes are accomplished through political channels. The drama of these escapes lies not in the refugees' need to survive in the wilderness, or in the constant fear of recap-

ture; instead, the tension lies in the political machinations that surround the attempt to escape oppression. Among the best examples of this type of escape is the flight of the Jewish people from the Soviet Union in the second half of the twentieth century.

The Jews and the Soviet Union

A confederation of Russia, Ukraine, and many other states in eastern Europe and Asia, the Soviet Union was one of the largest and most powerful nations on Earth during much of the twentieth century. It was also one of the most oppressive. The government expounded a hard-line Communist ideology in which free elections were banned, and political power was instead wielded by a single dictator and a small group of advisers. The national government relied on an extensive network of secret police to monitor its citizens. It routinely stifled dissent, often sentencing people to prison merely for objecting to government policy, and it established a sluggish, mind-numbing bureaucracy that dominated civic life.

The Soviet government treated most of its citizens poorly, but it reserved special indignities for the country's Jewish population. Soviet Jews were expected to assimilate into the rest of Soviet society and were expressly discouraged from practicing their religion.

Those who tried to learn Hebrew, dress according to their religious dictates, or otherwise identify themselves as Jews were subject to harassment and arrest.

To be sure, the Soviets did not invent anti-Semitism, or prejudice against Jews. Most of the states that made up the Soviet Union had a long history of persecuting Jews. For centuries before the formation of the Soviet Union in 1917, hundreds of thousands of Jews had lived in the cities and small settlements of Russia, Lithuania, Ukraine, and other eastern European nations. In places, the Jewish population approached one quarter of the total. The Jews of the region

A mob of Russians assaults a Jew as police look on. Anti-Semitism made life difficult for many Russian Jews.

were shopkeepers, farmers, and scholars, and they had a long, proud tradition of devotedly following their religion.

All too often, however, the eastern European Jews were not welcomed by the Christians who were their neighbors. Jews do not believe in the divinity of Jesus Christ, a stance that many Christians of the time and place found impossible to tolerate. Moreover, Christian tradition had for many years blamed Jesus' crucifixion on the Jews. Although the event had taken place centuries earlier, European Christians continued to hold the Jews, as a people, responsible for the death of Jesus.

Jewish customs, too, from clothing to religious rituals, were often starkly different from those of the Christians. Most Jews avoided speaking Russian

A Jewish woman mourns her husband killed during a 1919 pogrom. Pogroms were designed to drive Jews out of the Soviet Union.

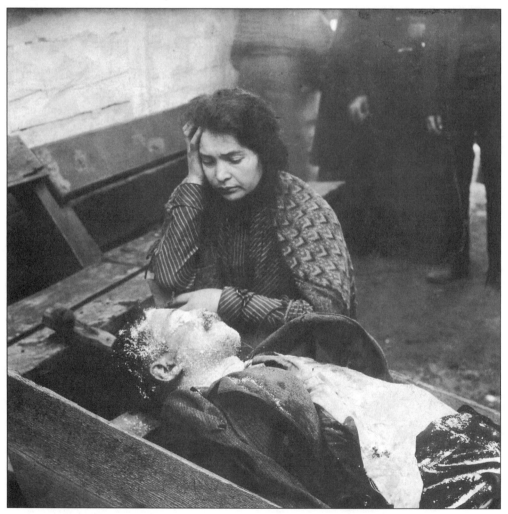

or other eastern European languages in favor of Hebrew or Yiddish, a language loosely based on German and used by many European Jews. Jews were seen by their neighbors as clannish and potentially dangerous. Indeed, Christians were usually prepared to believe the worst about the Jews. False rumors about Jewish conduct frequently spread throughout the region; one particularly damaging myth held that Jews used the blood of sacrificial Christian children in preparing their Passover meals.

Sometimes, these suspicions merely resulted in low-level harassment, in which Jews were teased, taunted, and occasionally beaten by neighbors and authorities. Sometimes, though, intolerance expressed itself more violently. Until World War I, pogroms, or state-sponsored persecutions, were common in many parts of Russia and other eastern European nations. During these attacks, soldiers would storm unexpectedly into Jewish settlements to destroy property, confiscate wealth, and kill. Hundreds of thousands of eastern European Jews lived in fear of being the next victims of an organized attack.

Jews and the Soviet Union

To a degree, the status of eastern Europe's Jews improved with the formation of the Soviet Union. Although anti-Jewish prejudice continued, especially on a local level, the excesses of the pre-Communist period were no longer in evidence. Some anti-Jewish laws were rescinded, and the pogroms largely came to an end. For the first time in

Pogroms and Emigration

Before the Soviet Union was founded, the Jews of eastern Europe often sought better lives in other lands. During the late nineteenth and early twentieth centuries, as many as 2 million Jews from future Soviet territories left their homes for other countries. Local Christians were generally quite happy to see the Jewish population depart; indeed, one purpose of the pogroms was to make life so difficult for the Jews that they saw no alternative but to leave. Some settled in the Middle East. Others traveled to the United States or western Europe. They were early examples of Jews who fled religious persecution in eastern Europe, but they would not be the last.

generations, Jews in the Soviet Union were not in constant danger of violent attacks by the government.

The early days of the Soviet Union held political and economic promise for the country's Jewish population, too. Many Jews approved of the new government's socialist orientation, believing that anti-Semitism would eventually disappear under a government in which all people, at least in theory, were held as equal. The new regime, moreover, brought the Jews of the Soviet Union job prospects and educational opportunities that had never been available to them.

But these benefits were a mirage. As time passed, it became evident that the

Soviet government was not friendly to Jewish interests. During the 1930s, the regime pushed for greater cohesion among the various Soviet peoples. Those who held onto traditional religious or cultural ideas were suddenly suspect, and the effect on Jews was particularly pronounced. The government quickly moved to limit Jewish prospects in business, government, and education.

The effects of this move were widespread and permanent. Jewish bureaucrats and military officers were inexplicably fired or demoted. Jewish students found it harder to secure a place at a university; Jewish academics lost their teaching posts or saw the size of their research grants cut sharply while non-Jews were given full funding. Soviet authorities dismissed Jewish concerns about these new policies. One official document mockingly characterized Jewish objections as an endless series of trivial, paranoid complaints. But to the victims of anti-Semitic bias, the changes were hardly inconsequential.

"No Place for Soviet Youngsters"

In the years after World War II, Soviet Jews increasingly began to realize that Communist persecution was not only hampering their economic progress; it was costing them their religious and cultural identity as well. The Soviet state was officially atheist and had a deep hostility to organized religion, particularly Judaism. As part of an effort to eradicate Judaism, the government shut down most Soviet syna-

gogues. Although a few did remain open, they were carefully monitored by Soviet police, and authorities discouraged citizens from attending services. "The synagogue," insisted one official, "is no place for Soviet youngsters."[27]

Most other expressions of Jewish religious and cultural life were forbidden as well. After 1948, no books were published in Yiddish anywhere in the country, and the last remaining Jewish theater in Moscow was permanently shut the following year. One Leningrad man was fined for "organizing an illegal meeting of a religious community"[28] simply for trying to discuss the meaning of the Jewish Sabbath with a group of friends. Ownership of most sacred texts was banned. Even Bibles were difficult to find.

As time went on, too, Soviet Jews found themselves at serious risk. Hundreds were arrested on charges of anti-Soviet behavior, a catchall term that covered everything from inciting riots to wearing a Star of David, the symbol of Judaism, in public; in most cases, the crimes amounted to nothing more than speaking out against anti-Semitism or reading a forbidden book. Nearly all of those arrested were found guilty and sentenced to prison terms. Many were shipped to labor camps in far-off Siberia, where conditions were deplorable. Some Jews were put to death.

A Reawakening

By the end of World War II, Soviet Jewish life had lost much of its distinctiveness. It was true that the pogroms

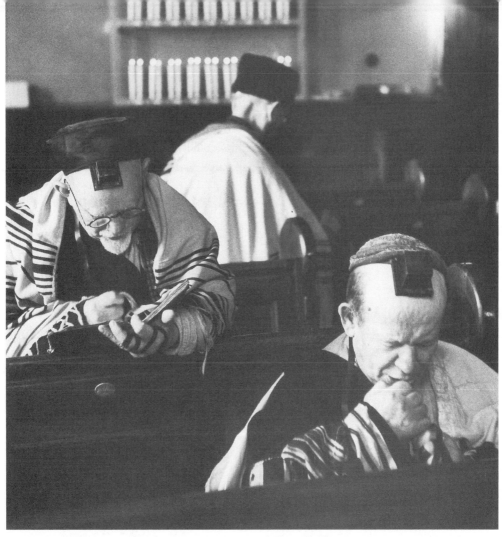

Orthodox Jews pray in a Moscow synagogue. After 1948 many Soviet Jews tried to obtain exit visas to emigrate to the new state of Israel.

had vanished, but so too had the small Jewish villages that had once been scattered across eastern Europe. The bulk of Jews now lived secular, assimilated lives in the cities and larger towns of the Soviet Union. Younger generations no longer studied Hebrew, and most Soviet Jews increasingly spoke Russian rather than Yiddish. "Here in the Soviet Union," one Soviet Jew complained, "[Jews] are indifferent to their culture and know nothing about their past."[29]

But despite its attempts to assimilate the nation's Jews, the Soviet government could not completely suppress interest in Jewish culture and religious practices. After World War II, in particular, small Jewish study groups sprang up in cities and towns across Soviet territory. Meeting in secret, these groups sought to learn about Judaism and Jewish ways. Sympathizers in other countries sent Bibles, Hebrew dictionaries, and other materials to help.

In some towns, Jews founded Jewish nursery and primary schools as well.

By Soviet law, the people who belonged to these groups were already Jewish: Indeed, their passports and other official papers identified them as such. Most Soviet Jews saw the designation as a source of shame rather than pride. Being Jewish, after all, was a serious handicap, both personally and professionally, in the Soviet Union. But as the members of these groups learned more about Jewish customs and religious doctrines, they became more positive about their Jewish identity. Increasingly, they were willing, even eager, to identify themselves as Jews.

The Israeli Option

In the years immediately following World War II, many of these Jews began to explore the possibility of leaving the Soviet Union altogether. Their goal was to reach another country where they could practice their religion as they chose and where their economic and educational opportunities would not be so limited. For some, the goal was the United States. For others, it was England or the nations of western Europe. But most Soviet Jews hoped to go to the newly established country of Israel.

Founded in 1948 on the recommendation of the United Nations, Israel had been created from British colonial holdings in the Middle East, the Jews' ancestral homeland. The new country promised to be a safe haven for the world's Jewish population. It was to be a Jewish state, where Jews would be in charge of the government and where Jewish culture and religious thought would be the foundation of daily life. For Soviet Jews who longed for religious liberty and a closer connection to Jewish culture, Israel seemed the answer to a prayer.

The question was how to get there. Soviet rulers severely limited emigration, allowing virtually no one to leave the country. Although exit visas—offi-

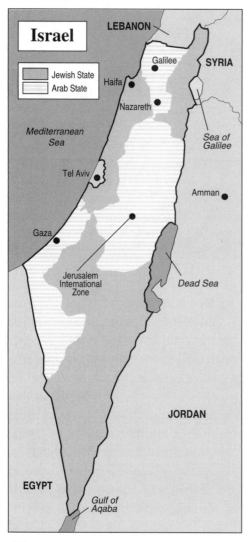

cial permissions to emigrate—were possible to obtain in theory, in practice they were awarded only in exceptional circumstances. Jewish scientist Yuri Tarnopolsky summed up the Soviet attitude toward emigration with this imaginary dialogue between a citizen and a government official:

"Do I have the right to leave the country?" "Yes, of course." "Great! Can I have an exit visa?" "By no means."[30]

The unavailability of exit visas stemmed from Communist ideology. Soviet leaders held that their socialist economy and political system helped all the nation's citizens. In their view, the Soviet Union had achieved a sort of workers' paradise. To have permitted people to leave would have been an admission that some Soviet citizens were not as satisfied with their lives as the official Communist line claimed them to be.

Soviet Jews were well aware of their country's antiemigration policies. Still, by 1948, the depth of the Soviet government's anti-Semitism had become obvious. Soviet Jews believed that the nation would be eager to be rid of them. However, they knew the government would not let them go to the United States or Western Europe—as longstanding enemies of the Soviet Union, such a move would be a public relations disaster for the Soviet government. But Israel was not aligned with the West, and in fact the Soviet Union had supported its founding. Allowing Jews to leave for Israel would not necessarily cause the Soviet Union to lose face.

Numbers

No one knows exactly how many Jews were living in the Soviet Union at any given moment. Although the Soviet Union conducted a regular census, the national government suppressed information it did not wish to be known and altered data to present a positive picture to the rest of the world. Most official counts after World War II put the total number of Soviet Jews at around 2 million; given these circumstances, however, such figures are very much open to question.

In particular, some observers and historians argue that the Soviet government deliberately underestimated the Jewish population, perhaps in an attempt to make the Jews seem even more of a minority—and therefore, even less important—than their actual numbers would indicate. In this view, a population of 3 million by midcentury is a more accurate estimate. And a few sources suggest an even higher figure—perhaps 5 million. No one will ever know for sure.

"A Soviet Citizen Should Be Ashamed"

Hopeful that the government would look favorably on their efforts to leave, hundreds of Soviet Jews now began trying to obtain an elusive exit visa. This was no easy assignment. The process was long, complex, cumbersome, and frequently demeaning. Bureaucrats shunted applicants from

Immigration officials check passports in Haifa, Israel. Obtaining documents to leave the Soviet Union was extremely difficult for Jews.

one office to another and demanded a seemingly unending series of documents from would-be emigrants. The slightest flaw in filling out a form often required an applicant to begin all over again.

The process was also a sham. The government permitted virtually none of these applicants to emigrate. Between 1948 and 1953, only a very small number of Jews—some sources say as few as six—were permitted to leave the country for Israel. And these Jews were hardly typical of the bulk of Soviet Jewry. They were without exception elderly and lived alone, with all their immediate relatives already in Israel as the result of emigration before the Soviet takeover. Young Jews, middle-aged Jews, Jews with jobs, Jews in the military, Jews with family in the Soviet Union—none were given permission to leave.

The truth was that the Soviet government had no interest in permitting emigration, even for Jews. In part, Soviet leaders banned Jewish emigration simply because they could. Theirs was a regime, after all, built largely on repression and intimidation. But mostly, the Soviets turned down the applicants for the same reason that they banned virtually all emigration: because they viewed leaving the country as a betrayal of all that the Soviet state stood for. The very notion of emigration was anti-Soviet, and in a self-described workers' paradise, not even the "lowly" Jews were expendable. When one potential emigrant asked a government official about the chances of going to Israel, the official replied, "A Soviet citizen should be ashamed to ask such a question."[31]

In Search of a Visa

Those Jews denied permission to leave the country in the late 1940s were disappointed, and often devastated, that their requests were not approved. But the inability to emigrate was not their only punishment. In most cases, the Soviet government took retribution against those who had applied. Many would-be emigrants were arrested and sent to prison camps. The rest were subjected to harassment and discrimination. In Soviet eyes, simply requesting permission to emigrate was a crime, and government officials responded accordingly.

Given the refusals and the oppressive policies directed at prospective emigrants, the Soviet Jews had several options. One was to give up the dream of emigration, and in the short run, at least, this was certainly the safest option. In this scenario, Soviet Jews would resign themselves to life in an anti-Semitic nation. They would do their best to practice their faith without attracting attention—or they would double their efforts to assimilate.

Another more dangerous option was to try to slip undetected across the border. This method, however, was impossible for most Jews. The great bulk of Soviets lived hundreds of miles from the nearest national boundary. Moreover, Soviet officials limited citizens' movements and knew if someone was heading toward a border without permission. While a handful of Jews did try this method of escape, few, if any, were successful.

But there was a third possibility: continuing to agitate for the right to go to Israel. This was in some ways the riskiest option of all. Soviet leaders had already demonstrated their unwillingness to permit emigration, along with their determination to punish those who tried. Yet for many Soviet Jews, the benefits of fighting for their religious freedom seemed to outweigh the risks. From the early 1950s until the collapse of the Soviet empire in the early 1990s, hundreds of thousands of Soviet Jews applied for exit visas.

The Refuseniks

These applications functioned in part as a symbol of Jewish resistance to the Soviet government. Each rejection served to remind other Soviet Jews of their oppression. Each refusal to per-

mit an applicant to emigrate encouraged other Jews to join the dissent. The applications also had an effect on the Soviet Union's reputation among other nations. The sheer number of people who applied to leave made it difficult for the regime to pretend that the country's Jews were fully satisfied with Soviet life.

But the applications were not merely symbolic. By requesting exit visas again and again; by making their wish-

Thousands gather in New York City in 1975 to support the rights of Soviet Jews to emigrate to Israel and to practice Judaism.

es and frustrations known in Israel, the United States, and other countries; and by holding firm to what they believed, the Soviet Jews hoped to convince their government to let them go.

It was, of course, a dangerous decision. Like those who had asked to leave directly after Israel's founding, those who tried to emigrate later on were vulnerable to added persecution. Mathematician Ilya Essas lost his job almost as soon as he submitted his application. Scientist Yuri Tarnopolsky was one of thousands of Soviet Jews imprisoned after being denied an exit visa.

Still, the applicants did not give in. Upon being rejected, many Soviet Jews simply began the process again. Some would-be emigrants were rejected two, three, or even more times. One dissident, Leonid Kelbert, was told by an official that he would "never, never, *never* be allowed to leave the country."[32] Others were informed that they would die in the Soviet Union, no matter how many times they applied. Yet thousands of would-be emigrants paid no attention.

Those who had been turned away became known as *refuseniks*. Many in this category bore the title with a certain pride. "I asked for a visa louder [the second time]," said one man, "and I want everyone who meets me to say louder that I cannot get permission to go."[33] In his eyes, being a refusenik helped to further the cause of the Soviet Jews. The more attention he could draw to Soviet restrictions on emigration and religious freedom, he believed, the better.

Publicity and Other Nations

In fact, the refuseniks' ability to publicize their plight was critical. Although refuseniks' phone calls were monitored and their mail was often intercepted, friends and family members in North America, western Europe, and Israel soon learned the facts of Jewish life in the Soviet Union. Some of these foreigners arranged to take trips to the Soviet Union for the purpose of seeing the situation firsthand. At times they were able to talk directly with refuseniks. Most came back from their trips impressed by the sincerity and strength of the dissidents. American rabbi Albert S. Axelrad, who visited the Soviet Union in 1978, spoke for many when he described the refuseniks as "voices of struggle and hope [who] will not be denied."[34]

Long before Axelrad's visit, though, organizations had formed in many different countries to support the Soviet Union's Jewish population. These groups educated the people of their own nations about the situation in the Soviet Union. They also tried to influence Soviet leaders to permit the Jews to leave. A Chicago organization, for example, printed and distributed postcards calling on the Soviets to allow Yuri Tarnopolsky to leave for Israel; more than five thousand of these cards were sent to Moscow by people across the world. Similar campaigns were waged on behalf of other refuseniks.

In some cases, requests for help reached foreign politicians and government officials. Canadian foreign minister Lester Pearson and U.S. senator Paul Simon were two of many who made a point of inquiring into the status of the refuseniks when they met with Soviet leaders. In 1974, Congress passed an amendment to a bill offering the Soviets trade advantages with the United States in exchange for liberalized emigration policies for Soviet Jews. And a group of Jews in the Soviet Republic of Georgia appealed directly to the United Nations for assistance in 1969, winning promises of support from members of the organization's Human Rights Commission.

Meanwhile, the Jews of the Soviet Union continued to agitate for their freedom at home. As the years passed, the demands for emigration became louder—and more reckless. In 1969, for instance, Dora Zak of Latvia renounced her Soviet citizenship after repeated refusals. "For nearly twenty years," she wrote in a letter to Soviet officials, "I have been subject to incessant moral and material deprivation, the only reason for which is the fact that I am a Jew."[35] Although renouncing her citizenship made her subject to almost certain arrest, Zak was not the only dissident to take this step.

Jews became bolder, too, in speaking out in support of one another. In 1971, several Jewish dissidents went on trial in Moscow on charges of anti-Soviet agitation. The arrests prompted a group of refuseniks to send a letter to government leaders. "The aim of the trials," the group argued, "is to carry out yet another reprisal against Jews who wish

to live in Israel and to frighten those who seek to depart. . . . We demand that [the prisoners] be released and granted exit visas."[36] The words and sentiments of such letters were far stronger than they were during the 1950s.

Even before these episodes, though, the early trickle of applications to emigrate had become a flood. Soviet Jews were increasingly eager to leave—and increasingly willing to risk everything to do so. In 1967, Soviet Jewish journalist Leonid Finkelstein estimated that about half the country's Jews had at least looked into applying for an exit visa. Even those who consider this figure too high concede that the numbers of those trying to emigrate had risen steeply since the early 1950s. And interest continued to grow through the 1970s and 1980s as well.

"An Unbelievable Amount of Red Tape"

The dissidents were helped in their quest by the Soviet Union's status as one of the world's most influential countries. Oppressive as the Soviet Union could be, it was very much a member of the world community of nations, particularly after Premier Joseph Stalin's death in 1953. The leaders who succeeded Stalin hoped to represent their country as kind and benevolent. While they had no compunction about sending dissidents to prison camps, denying civil rights for their citizens, or flatly refusing emigration requests, they preferred to carry out these activities in secret rather than in the public eye.

Jewish women at the Russian Embassy in England protest the trials of Jews in Moscow in 1971. Several Jews were charged with engaging in anti-Soviet activities.

For this reason, the refuseniks' constant agitation helped them, as did the efforts on their behalf by the people of other nations. The more public the complaints, the less the Soviets could afford to ignore them. Beginning in 1953, the Soviets allowed certain numbers of Jews to emigrate nearly every year. The figures were quite small at first. Probably no more than a thousand Soviet Jews left for Israel during the 1950s; like their predecessors, most of the 1950s emigrants were retired and had children in the Middle East. But as

time passed, the numbers began to grow. By 1970, more than ten thousand Soviet Jews had been given official permission to emigrate.

The number of exit visas granted, to be sure, was only a small percentage of the total of applications. Nearly all who sought to escape were turned down. Some were refused because as scientists or military personnel, they were deemed to be in possession of state secrets. Others were denied permission because they were leaders of the pro-emigration movement or because

Soviet Jews attempt to get past a guard to speak to Israeli representatives at the Dutch embassy in Moscow in 1990.

they lacked close relatives in Israel. Most, though, were given no formal reason for their rejection.

Nor was it clear on what basis applications were accepted. The elderly continued to be the largest group of those allowed to leave, but a smattering of younger people received permission to emigrate as well. Some with parents or children in Israel were accepted; others, in exactly the same situation, were denied. Yuri Tarnopolsky

was allowed to emigrate soon after being released from a long prison term, while others with equally long sentences were refused. The process was arbitrary and seemingly capricious.

Moreover, the Soviet government made escape as difficult as possible for those Jews who did receive permission to flee the country. Government officials imposed a burdensome exit tax, for instance, on those who wished to emigrate. For a time the government instituted a diploma tax, too, requiring that those with college educations repay the cost of their schooling. Those granted permission were typically given three weeks to leave the country. Refusenik Mark Azbel recalled "cop[ing] with an unbelievable amount of red tape"[37] during his last days as a Soviet citizen—much of it designed simply to punish him for choosing to leave.

Soviet officials also interfered with family relationships in ways that can only be considered vindictive. Some parents were given exit visas—but their teenage children were not. One member of a married couple would be given permission to emigrate, while the other was refused again and again. In 1974, Avital Stieglitz, who was engaged to marry refusenik Anatoly Shcharansky, was given a visa that expired the day after her wedding. She married and left immediately for Israel; it would be twelve years before her husband was permitted to join her.

Russian president Vladimir Putin (left) and Israeli prime minister Ehud Barak shake hands. By 1992 restrictions on emigration for Russian Jews had eased considerably.

The 1970s and Afterward

But despite the roadblocks to emigration, the continued oppression of those who spoke out, and the seemingly random nature of the approvals, it was clear by the end of the 1960s that the refuseniks had made a difference. Through their steadfastness, their courage, and their willingness to take risks, thousands of Jews had escaped the religious persecution of the Soviet Union.

Nor did the late 1960s mark the high point of their work. On the contrary, the numbers of emigrants generally increased as time went on. In 1973 alone, almost thirty-five thousand Soviet Jews were allowed to leave the country. In 1979, the total was over fifty thousand. To be sure, there were years in which world events or internal conflict made the Soviets crack down more sharply on the Jewish dissidents. In 1984, for instance, fewer than a thousand Jews were permitted to emigrate.

Still, the overall trend was clear. Little by little, the refuseniks were managing to flee the Soviet Union. Those who had been told they would never see Israel found themselves on flights to the Middle East. Jews who had longed to emigrate, but had never dared to apply, now filed for exit visas—and, increasingly, received them on the first try. By the late 1980s, in fact, the gates had opened so wide that emigration had become almost simple. Between 1989 and the end of the Soviet empire in 1992, nearly half a million Jews fled the Soviet Union.

Courage and Strength

The escape of the Jews is attributable in part to the interest and support of people elsewhere in the world. Their refusal to let the Soviet treatment of Jews go unnoticed shamed Soviet leaders and interfered with government policies. In some cases, such as those of Anatoly Shcharansky and Yuri Tarnopolsky, foreign protests led directly to the release of dissidents. At the very least, the concern of other countries helped immeasurably in bolstering the spirits of the refuseniks.

But the escapes were fundamentally the work of the Soviet Jews themselves. They were the ones who risked their careers, their families, and their lives for the right to emigrate; they were the ones who fought to keep their plight in the public eye. They showed tremendous courage and strength in fighting for what they believed. And through it all, they kept alive their hope and their faith. Even those who had been rejected time and again never lost sight of their ultimate goal. As one longtime refusenik optimistically told a visiting foreign journalist, "You are invited to my house—in Israel."[38]

4

The Mormons
Move West

THE HISTORY OF the nineteenth century in America is in large part the story of westward expansion. The men and women who moved across the Mississippi and toward the Pacific Coast did so for various reasons. For many, the draw was economic. In parts of the West, the government offered settlers free land; others searched for gold or took steadier if less potentially lucrative jobs herding cattle, catching fish, or cutting lumber. Still others went west in search of adventure. And some, wearying of the increasingly urban East, were attracted to the West for its scenery, climate, and open spaces.

But one of the largest and most important journeys to the West was sparked by something else entirely. In 1846, thousands of members of a reli-gious organization known as the Mormon Church set out from Illinois on a journey to the Utah desert, where they planned to build a new community on the shores of the Great Salt Lake. Church members had suffered from persecution everywhere they had settled. Their journey to Utah was an attempt to find a safe haven from which no further escape would be necessary.

The Founding of Mormonism

The Mormon Church, officially known as the Church of Jesus Christ of Latter-day Saints, was founded in 1830 by Joseph Smith of western New York State, but its roots go back to 1820. That year, according to Smith's account, he began having visions in which God, Jesus Christ, or one of several angels appeared to him. Over the next ten years, these visions appeared to him frequently.

At first, Smith's visions rested on images that would have been familiar and

An angel leads Joseph Smith to the tablets that would be translated as The Book of Mormon.

acceptable to most Christians of the time. But over the years, the visions carried Smith further and further away from mainstream Christian thinking. In one of Smith's revelations, for example, an angel led him to a set of golden tablets buried on a New York hillside. These tablets, explained the angel, contained hieroglyphic writings that described the history of the ancient dwellers of New York. According to Smith's account, these ancient peoples were in reality the descendants of lost Hebrew tribes mentioned in the Bible. They had reached the New World in about 600 B.C., where they constructed a complex, sophisticated society—only to see it destroyed by war.

Like the people in the Old World, these New World residents knew about Jesus Christ. But the New World version of Christianity, Smith believed, was truer and purer than the Old World expression of the religion. Besides, the tablets assured Smith that the next coming of Jesus would be in the New World—but only after Smith had established a true Christian church in North America.

With guidance from the angels in his visions, Smith translated the tablets and published them as *The Book of Mormon* in 1830. Many Americans found themselves drawn to Mormon doctrine. As expressed in its acceptance of modern-day prophets and the expectation of Jesus' swift return, Mormonism had an immediacy and a relevance that traditional Christianity could not match. Moreover, Smith was a charismatic man. By early 1831, less than a year after the publication of *The Book of Mormon*, the church already numbered about six hundred members, and it would grow dramatically in the next dozen years.

Oppression Begins

But the rise of the Mormon faith came at a cost. Most mainstream Christians objected to the tenets of Mormonism. They found Smith's notions ludicrous, dangerous, and simply wrong, and they scorned and mocked those who accepted the new doctrines. Most converts joined the group over the objections of families and friends. Poet John Greenleaf Whittier dismissed those who embraced Mormonism as "weak hearts, tossed and troubled,"[39] and some writers were a good deal more blunt in their descriptions.

The structure of the Mormon Church also raised doubts and suspicions among nonmembers (who were called "gentiles" by the Mormons). Outsiders perceived the Mormons as clannish and arrogant, with little interest in those around them. Moreover, the Mormons were reluctant to share details of their rituals and doctrines with nonmembers. This secrecy convinced many observers that church leaders were less interested in saving souls than in brainwashing members.

To a degree, these accusations were valid. The Mormons were indeed a tightly knit community, and they did have rituals and doctrines that they chose to hide from their neighbors. On the other hand, it is not hard to understand why they acted as they did. Nineteenth-century Protestant America was noted for religious intolerance. Knowing that their doctrines were rejected by the community around them, Mormons were uncertain whether their neighbors would prove trustworthy. Under those circumstances, banding together around a shared faith was not only reasonable but necessary.

Joseph Smith had anticipated that his group would be mistreated by non-Mormons, and very early on he took steps to find a safe haven where Mormonism could flourish. Leaving the settled Northeast behind, he led his followers west to Kirtland, Ohio, where he hoped to establish a holy city where his fellow Mormons could live in peace.

But the Mormons quickly drew the ire of their new Ohio neighbors. Before long, intolerance had driven the Mormons west again, this time to a site near Independence, Missouri. There, reaction to the newcomers was even worse. Mobs tarred and feathered Mormon leaders. Smith was jailed on several trumped-up charges. Even Missouri's governor joined in the hysteria. "The Mormons," he said in 1838, "must be exterminated or driven from the state if necessary for the public peace."[40]

The governor of Missouri signs the 1838 order to expel Mormons from the state. The Mormons then moved their church to Illinois.

The Mormons were reluctant to give in to public pressure, but realistically they had little choice. In 1838, the group left Independence. Twice the Mormons had tried, and failed, to find a place of refuge in the settled eastern half of the country. The question now was whether such a haven actually existed.

Nauvoo

Even after two bad experiences, Joseph Smith was still eager to find a home for the Mormons. In the winter of 1839, the Mormons moved their church head-quarters to Commerce, Illinois. Located in the swampy lowlands just across the Mississippi River from southern Iowa, Commerce was a small, sleepy, and fever-ridden town. Shallow water and nearby rapids made it inaccessible to most river steamboats, and the town had no industry to speak of. Still, Smith had high hopes for the place.

The Mormons purchased the land from the few people who lived there and renamed the town Nauvoo. They drained the swamps, built streets, and carved out farms from nearby forests. Before long they began building a magnificent temple. The city grew quickly as converts from the East joined those who had fled Missouri. By 1844, Nauvoo had about twenty thousand inhabitants and ranked as one of the largest cities in the state. Within Nauvoo itself, the population was overwhelmingly Mormon. Outside the city's boundaries, meanwhile, newly arrived Mormons lived side by side with long-established Protestants.

At first, the Mormons were welcomed by the gentiles around Nauvoo. The farmers and townspeople of western Illinois believed that the group had been treated unfairly in Missouri and Ohio. The citizens of nearby Quincy, indeed, had funneled money and goods to Smith and his followers in their flight from Missouri. Moreover, the farmers and business leaders of the area thought they stood to benefit economically from the Mormon presence. More people, after all, would mean more markets for their goods and services.

But soon after the Mormons arrived, tensions began to grow. Just as in Ohio and Missouri, the people of western Illinois grew suspicious of Mormon religious ideas. In the summer of 1841, less than two years after Smith and his followers arrived, a group of county residents banded together and resolved to have "nothing to do [with] the peculiar religious opinions of the people calling themselves Mormons."[41] The

Oppression in Ohio and Missouri

In both Ohio and Missouri, intolerance of the Mormons largely came from Christian opposition to Mormon religious doctrines and practices. The citizens of Kirtland and Independence objected to living in close quarters with this unfamiliar group. Local clergymen spent many of their sermons bitterly denouncing the Mormons and their religious practices. A Missouri newspaper editor, quoted in Paul Bailey's *The Armies of God*, spoke for many when he wrote scathingly of Mormon certainty "that they have wrought miracles, and have been the subjects of miraculous and supernatural cures, [and] have conversed with God and his angels."

Though religious differences were at the heart of the intolerance, the people of Ohio and Missouri had other objections to the Mormons, too. Some accused the newcomers of being thieves, an accusation that was not helped by Smith's peripheral involvement in an Ohio banking scandal. Missouri slaveholders viewed the Mormons' abolitionist sentiments with suspicion and disgust. And some argued that the Mormons were engaged in a political power play. In their eyes, the Mormon settlements were an attempt to gain a voting majority throughout the region, thereby putting political power in the hands of the church and its members. Each of these themes would play a role in the intolerance faced by Mormons in Nauvoo later on.

proclamation did concede that Mormons had the right to practice their religion as they saw fit; still, Mormons had not escaped religious intolerance even here.

It soon became clear to many Christians around Nauvoo that the Mormons, by virtue of their numbers, held a great deal of political power. Smith had talked Illinois government officials into granting Nauvoo a degree of self-government unknown elsewhere in the state, and county government was increasingly dominated by Mormons as well. To the gentiles of the region, it seemed clear that the Mormons spoke with one voice—a voice opposed to anyone who was not a Mormon.

There was another concern as well: the Nauvoo Legion. This was a privately financed Mormon militia, paid for by the church and consisting only of church members. The army, Smith said, was purely for defensive purposes, and indeed it never showed any sign of attacking Nauvoo's neighbors. Still, the people in the area were uncomfortable with the legion's size and power. The gentiles of western Illinois wondered if the church's true aim was to replace representative democracy with government of, by, and for the Mormons. As one observer wrote, "These Mormons are accumulating like a snowball rolling down an inclined plane, which in the end becomes an avalanche."[42]

Brigham Young's wives sit behind their husband as he preaches. Many people felt the Mormon practice of polygamy was immoral.

Polygamy

Both religious doctrine and political considerations had sparked anti-Mormon sentiment in Ohio and Missouri, and now they were doing the same in Illinois. The Mormon experience in Nauvoo, however, introduced a new point of conflict as well. This was polygamy, or the practice of a man taking more than one wife at a time.

During the early nineteenth century, polygamy was practically unknown in the United States. It was not only illegal; it was also commonly considered immoral by Christians. Smith, however, cited the prophets and kings of the Old Testament, many of whom had many wives, and decreed that polygamy was acceptable among Mormons. At first, aware that this custom might spark the fury of his gentile neighbors, he kept the doctrine a secret within the community.

But polygamy did not remain a secret for long. In 1844, a group of dissatisfied Mormons specifically mentioned polygamy in a published exposé of church practices. Though Smith tried to confiscate the group's writings, the damage had been done. The knowledge that Mormons sanctioned polygamy angered most gentiles of western Illinois. For some, the revelation simply added fuel to already existing anti-Mormon feeling. Others who had been neutral or even supportive now found themselves in opposition to the Mormons as well.

The Mob Forms

The result was a dramatic change in the level of hostility toward Mormons.

Mobs began to torment Mormons who lived outside Nauvoo. Victimized by arson, gunshots, and threats both spoken and silent, those in outlying areas soon fled their homes for the safety of the city. Nauvoo itself increasingly took on the characteristics of a community under siege. The Nauvoo Legion drilled feverishly, and Smith exhorted his followers to stand firm against their oppressors. The Mormons, he said, "shall have their legal rights and shall be protected from mob violence. . . . While I live, I will never tamely submit to the dominion of cursed mobocracy."[43]

Finally some gentiles called for Smith's arrest on charges of treason. Fearing that war would break out between the Nauvoo Legion and anti-Mormon agitators, Illinois governor Thomas Ford urged Smith to surrender. If Smith gave himself up, Ford reasoned, the mob might be calmed long enough to avoid violence. Moreover, the governor pointed out, Smith might well be safer in a prison cell than roaming the streets of Nauvoo. In June 1844, Smith, reluctantly agreeing, traveled to nearby Carthage, where he was imprisoned in the county jail.

But Ford had underestimated the depth of anti-Mormon feeling. Three days after Smith reported to prison, a screaming mob—made up in part of members of the state militia—stormed the jail. Smith was shot at least twice by the crowd. Then four men shot him again to make sure he was dead. Across much of Illinois, the assassination was greeted with enthusiasm. "THREE

CHEERS to the brave company that shot him to pieces!"[44] cried one Christian minister when he heard the news.

Fleeing to Safety

Despite the mob violence that had taken their leader, the Mormons of Nauvoo were not yet ready to leave their homes. Nauvoo, after all, was their holy city, their refuge, and the site of their still unfinished temple, so for religious reasons they were reluctant to abandon it. "Our temple must be completed," said Smith's successor, Brigham Young. "Take up your duties and carry on."[45]

The Mormons had economic justification to stay, as well. The buildings and land in and around Nauvoo represented several years of hard work. The Mormons had created prosperity where none had existed; by now, Nauvoo was one of the wealthier communities in the state. Church members did not relish the idea of leaving this valuable property behind, and there was no guarantee of getting a fair price for their land, homes, and businesses if they were suddenly forced to leave.

But while the Mormons determined to hang on, gentile violence against the newcomers did not diminish. Men from communities near Nauvoo formed a militia to arrest Mormons they thought were thieves; only the intervention of the governor got the militia to disband. Increasingly, too, even gentiles who did not actively oppose the Mormon presence were receiving threats. The non-

Mormon postmaster of one town was forced to escape a mob by slipping out his back door and paddling a canoe across the Mississippi to Iowa.

For the eighteen months following Smith's murder, the Mormons of Nauvoo resisted their neighbors' oppression. But the level of hostility only increased. By the fall of 1845, it was clear that the Mormons could not remain where they were without some sort of civil war breaking out. Mormon officials bowed to reality. In October 1845, they signed a letter promising to leave the next spring.

At first, the timetable seemed acceptable to the area's non-Mormons. By delaying the move till the spring, the Mormons would benefit from better weather than they would have if they left immediately. Moreover, the delay would allow them to sell their properties and wrap up their affairs in Nauvoo. Mormon church leaders began making arrangements for the community's migration west. They divided the city's residents into cooperative groups and ordered artisans to build wagons, while women sewed tents and extra clothing for the upcoming trek.

But some local gentiles were unwilling to wait. By this time, they did not want so much to be rid of the Mormons as to destroy them altogether. In December 1845, several months before the exodus was to begin, a federal agent came to Nauvoo with a warrant for Brigham Young's arrest on false charges of counterfeiting. Young managed to evade the officer, but rumors soon began that other federal and state officials would be on their way to Nauvoo well before springtime—and that they would not be content with arresting just one of the church's leaders.

Across the Mississippi

Despite the lack of preparation and the bitter winter weather, the Mormons acted quickly. Dozens of Nauvoo residents hurried to pack up as many of their possessions as they could fit on wagons and carts. Getting a fair price for their property was no longer a concern. Now, safety was the primary issue. As the winter progressed, in fact, the anger of the gentiles seemed to grow. Many of the residents who packed up first were church leaders fleeing the possibility of arrest. Others were women whose husbands were eager to have them out of town in case anti-Mormon violence should suddenly erupt.

By early February 1846, the first group had finished making their preparations for the trip west. To their disappointment, most had failed to sell their properties for anything like their actual value. One woman reported later that she was offered just eighteen dollars for her house and lot, which she considered was worth at least three hundred dollars. Still, the potential danger of waiting outweighed most Mormons' desires to recoup their investments.

A group of Mormons moves their belongings during a harsh winter storm after being driven from their community in Nauvoo, Illinois.

Faced with the possibility of arrest or violence, very few chose to remain in hopes of getting a better offer. On February 4, the first wagonload of refugees left Nauvoo for the refuge of Sugar Creek, Iowa, a small community about ten miles west of Nauvoo. "We left our home before we were ready to start on our journeying," wrote Jane Richards, "for the mob was so threatening that I dared not remain longer."[46]

Over the next few weeks, several thousand Mormons made their way to Sugar Creek. A few of these refugees moved out of Nauvoo in stages. William Clayton, for instance, spent a week shipping his family's goods across the river before he left Nauvoo altogether. But most of the city's Mormons made their escape to Sugar Creek as quickly as possible. Patty Bartlett Sessions's family, for instance, packed on February 10 and crossed the river two days later. Their experience was typical.

Unfortunately, the weather slowed down some of the escapees. There were no bridges across the Mississippi, so the travelers were forced to make their way across the river itself. The early February weather created ice chunks across the river's surface, which made it difficult to maneuver a boat from one shore to the other. Charles Shumway, the first to cross the river, drove his wagon directly onto a flatboat, which crossed to Iowa without incident, but he was lucky. After sending his goods across, William Clayton was stranded for nearly a week on the Illinois side of

the Mississippi. "Very cold and windy," he wrote in his journal. "Impossible to cross the river."[47]

Later in the month, however, the cold worked to the Mormons' advantage. When the low temperatures caused the river to freeze solid, some Nauvoo residents were able to drive their wagons directly across the frozen surface. This journey was easier and less frightening than trying to pilot a boat among floating pieces of ice.

Hardships

Regardless of how it was made, the trek to Iowa was dangerous. At least one boat suddenly sank about halfway across the Mississippi. Several passengers might well have died of exposure or drowning, but the others reacted quickly. Recognizing that her baby brother was trapped in a submerged pile of bedclothes, for instance, seven-year-old Eliza Ann Grover went to his rescue. "She immediately plunged down into the deep water," wrote Eliza Ann's sister afterwards, "[and] caught the babe by his dress by one hand."[48] Then she used the other hand to pull herself to safety.

Nor did conditions improve much at Sugar Creek. Patty Sessions and her family did without a tent for the first two weeks. Even those who had shelter found the accommodations appalling. "I cannot forget how cold I was standing in the tent preparing food and washing dishes for our big family," recalled Lucy Meserve Smith. "When I would wash a dish and raise it out of

A wagon train slowly makes its way across rocky terrain. The Mormon trek west was very dangerous and full of hardships.

the water there would be ice on it before I could get it wiped."[49]

Although many of the emigrants deeply missed their old lives in Nauvoo, for the most part they understood why they had needed to leave. The oppression in Illinois had simply been too overwhelming. William Clayton hoped that the journey out of Nauvoo would lead the Mormons to a place where, at last, they would "not be under the dominion of gentile governments, subject to the wrath of mobs."[50] And many asserted that the prevailing mood in Sugar Creek was thankfulness at having successfully made their escape.

The Way West

As the spring continued, more and more citizens of Nauvoo hurried west.

Hardships on the Trail

The Mormons who traveled west from Winter Quarters with Brigham Young were encouraged to press on by the prospect of finding a place where they could practice their religion freely. Their optimism in achieving this goal carried them through some very difficult times. On June 19, 1847, for instance, the group came to a spot that William Clayton described as follows, from his book *William Clayton's Journal:*

> This is considered by all to be the worst camping ground we have had on the journey. . . . There is some grass in this place for our teams but no wood. The brethren [fellow Mormons] have to make use of the wild sage and buffalo chips [dried buffalo dung] to do their cooking. There are two small streams of water, one appears to come from the northwest and is not very bad water; the other is from the southwest and is so bad that cattle will not drink it. It is strong of salt or rather saleratus [baking soda] and smells extremely filthy. Its banks are so perfectly soft that a horse or ox cannot go down to drink without sinking immediately nearly overhead [above its head] in thick, filthy mud, and is one of the most horrid, swampy, stinking places I ever saw. . . . The mosquitoes are very bad indeed at this place which adds to the loathsome, solitary scenery around.

By mid-June, one Mormon official wrote that the city was virtually deserted. The mobs, however, only increased the level of their hostility toward the few Mormons who remained. Earlier, they had shied away from entering Nauvoo, but now they carried their persecutions into the heart of the city. By October, the last of the Mormons had escaped across the Mississippi. Nauvoo had been abandoned to the gentiles.

By this time, though, the first group of Mormons had moved on from Sugar Creek. Although the town had been a temporary place of refuge for church members, it was far too close to Nauvoo to be a permanent home. Illinois, Missouri, and Ohio had failed the Mormons; now, Brigham Young and other church leaders decided to go where there were no other settlers. They proposed journeying far to the west, perhaps as far as the Rocky Mountains. And so, throughout the summer of 1846, the refugees gradually made their way west across southern Iowa.

This part of the journey was no better than the hurried flight across the Mississippi. Roads were poor and often nonexistent; wagons stuck in thick prairie grass and bogged down in swamps. "Cloudy mud so deep we can hardly stir,"[51] reported Patty Sessions. The summer heat alternated with torrential rains, and disease was rampant.

Food and other supplies were hard to come by, too. Often the travelers had to stop for a week or more while the men found work on farms across the border in northern Missouri. These stops were a risk. The state was strongly anti-Mormon, and some of the Mormon leaders were still officially subject to arrest in Missouri. However, there seemed to be no alternatives. The travelers needed not only food for themselves but also feed for their oxen and horses. These needs kept the procession moving slowly. As the summer wore on, the group broke into smaller units; it proved impossible for everyone to stay together.

By the late fall, most of the Mormons had covered only a few hundred miles. With the Rocky Mountains still a long way off, the travelers settled down for the winter. Those at the head of the group stopped at a place known as Winter Quarters, along the Missouri River on the border between Iowa and Nebraska. Others, moving more slowly, stopped where they were along the trail in Iowa.

The Mormons had more time to prepare for the winter of 1846–1847 than they had had the previous year in Sugar Creek, and they quickly set to work to make the best of their circumstances. Winter Quarters, in particular, turned out surprisingly well given that the Mormons arrived just six weeks before the snow began to fall. "A city of at least 400 houses had been erected in a short space of time, through the ingenuity and industry of the Saints [Mormons],"[52] wrote one traveler with evident pride.

Still, the houses were makeshift and temporary; they served only to keep out the worst of the winter weather. In Winter Quarters as well as across much of Iowa, food was scarce, and feed for the animals almost nonexistent. Many travelers lacked warm clothing and sufficient fuel. Journal entries for the winter refer occasionally to music, worship, and other pastimes, but mostly, they describe bitter cold, hard work, and feelings of despair.

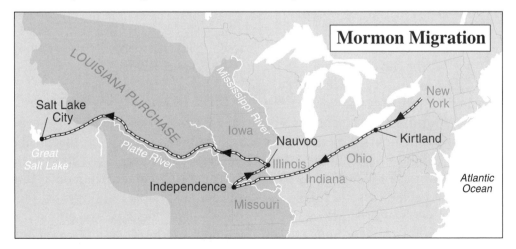

Mormon Migration

Brigham Young announces his selection of Utah's Great Salt Lake as the site for a permanent Mormon settlement.

In some ways, this was the hardest period for those Mormons who had fled Nauvoo. By February 1847, most of the refugees had been on the move for a full year. The comforts of Nauvoo seemed only a memory, yet they were still miles from their destination. But even Nebraska, which would not become a state for another twenty years, was too close to the settled East for the Mormons to risk making a permanent settlement along the Missouri River.

"This Is the Place"

Having come this far in their escape from religious persecution, though, the travelers knew there was no going back. When spring came, Brigham Young formed a group of almost 150 pioneers—including three women and two children—to head west in search of a spot where they could worship as they chose. The group left in April and traveled along Nebraska's Platte River into southern Wyoming, then turned southwest. They crossed mountains, rivers, and deserts; the going was often difficult, but they continued to reach deeper into the wilderness.

On July 24, the group reached the Great Salt Lake in northern Utah. Although there was little timber in the valley, the land was green and good for farming. Tired but excited, the travelers turned to Brigham Young. Though he was sick with a fever, Young carefully studied the area through a gap in the curtains of his wagon. After a few moments, Young rendered his verdict. "This is the place,"[53] he announced.

And indeed it was. At last, there was good news for the wandering Mormons. Forced to escape three times from the settled and intolerant East, they had found a refuge and home here in the western wilderness. The Mormon pioneers immediately started constructing farms and building Salt Lake City, a new holy city that would be larger and grander even than Nauvoo. Over the next few years, thousands of Mormons would arrive in the city—relieved and delighted to be safe at last. Patty Sessions spoke for many when she wrote, "My heart flows with gratitude to God that we have got home. . . . Have been blessed with life and health. I rejoice all the time."[54]

5

The Flight of the Dalai Lama

THE CENTRAL ASIAN country of Tibet is one of the least accessible places on Earth. Situated largely on windy plateaus amid the Himalayan mountains, the sparsely populated land lies far above sea level. The average altitude of the country is fifteen thousand feet, or nearly three miles—an elevation higher than any mountaintop in the contiguous United States. Some Tibetan villages are nearly sixteen thousand feet high, and even the capital city, Lhasa, lies at an elevation of more than twelve thousand feet.

Yet despite the altitude and the forbidding mountains, the history of Tibet is not one of total isolation. The nation often had to struggle to maintain its independence in the face of foreign rulers and powerful armies. That was partic-ularly true in the case of China, which borders Tibet to the east. On several occasions over the years, Chinese armies threatened Tibet's sovereignty—or conquered it entirely.

One of the worst of these occupations took place during the twentieth century. In the early 1950s, the Communist Chinese army swept into Tibet, meeting with little resistance from the small Tibetan forces. Hostile to Tibetan culture and particularly to the Buddhist religion prevalent in Tibet, Chinese officials attempted to solidify their hold on the country by capturing the Dalai Lama, the highest-ranking priest in the country and the spiritual leader of Tibet's people. What followed was one of the most dangerous and dramatic escapes of any religious leader in history.

Tibetan Buddhism and the Dalai Lama

Since the seventh century A.D., most Tibetans have followed the Buddhist faith. Over the years, though, Buddhism has developed in somewhat different ways in Tibet than it has in other countries. One of the most obvious distinctions of Tibetan Buddhism involves the role and prevalence of the country's priests, known in Tibet as lamas. Lamas are holy men, expected to be celibate, who live in monasteries and devote their time to meditation and good works. It has long been traditional for Tibetan families to send at least one son to the monasteries, and some estimates suggest that one out of every four Tibetan men through the ages has been a lama.

Buddhist monks blow ceremonial horns during a festival in Tibet. Tibetan lamas are spiritual leaders of the Buddhist faith.

Of all Tibetan lamas, the one known as the Dalai Lama is the most important. The Dalai Lama functions as the head of the Tibetan Buddhist religion and to a degree serves as the political leader of Tibet as well. Each succeeding Dalai Lama—to date, there have been fourteen in Tibetan history—is considered a different incarnation of the same soul; the doctrine of reincarnation, or rebirth, is central to Buddhist philosophy. This soul, known as Chenrezig, or Compassion, is believed to have already achieved the Buddhist goal of perfect understanding, but continues to be reborn in order to help other souls achieve enlightenment for themselves.

The belief that Chenrezig is perpetually being reborn makes finding each succeeding Dalai Lama difficult. According to Tibetan Buddhist theology, the next manifestation of Chenrezig can be any male of Tibetan ancestry born after the death of the previous Dalai Lama. There are no obvious and visible indications, such as being born into a wealthy or exceptionally pious family. Nor is Chenrezig necessarily reborn a predictable number of days following the former Dalai Lama's death.

The fourteenth Dalai Lama, for instance, was born into a poor family living on the edge of Tibet. Born in 1935, two years after the death of the previous Dalai Lama, he was given the name Lhamo Thondup at birth. From the beginning, his parents noticed some oddities about their child. His mother recalled, for instance, that Lhamo enjoyed putting his few belongings in

a box as part of his imaginative play. "He [said he] was packing to go to Lhasa," she remembered years later, "and would take all of us with him."[55]

Still, no one thought anything of such idiosyncrasies. His family never guessed that young Lhamo was the next manifestation of Chenrezig. But when the boy was three, a group of lamas from Lhasa entered his village in search of the newest Dalai Lama, who they believed was now growing up somewhere in Tibet. Various mystical signs had pointed them in the direction of Lhamo's family home—and finally to Lhamo himself.

After carrying out some tests, the members of the search party were certain that Lhamo was indeed the next Dalai Lama. "Our minds were filled with deep devotion, joy, and gaiety," recalled one of the searchers years afterward. "We were so moved that tears of happiness filled our eyes."[56] Before long, they had convinced Lhamo's astonished parents of his actual identity, arranged to bring him to Lhasa for training, and declared him the new incarnation of Chenrezig. As he had predicted through his creative play, Lhamo did indeed move to the Tibetan capital—and brought the rest of his family along.

The Threat from China

The first ten years of the new Dalai Lama's training were unremarkable. He lived a highly regimented life, much of it devoted to lessons in Buddhist philosophy, Tibetan culture, dialectics, and Tibetan debate. "I was a very reluctant pupil," he recalled years afterward, "and disliked all subjects equally."[57] There were also numerous religious ceremonies requiring the young leader's participation, and many hours were given over to prayer and meditation as well.

But the relative calm of the Dalai Lama's education masked the fact that he had arrived in Lhasa at a pivotal time in Tibetan history. Nearby China had claimed Tibet in the early 1900s. For many years following the claim, internal wars and dissension had kept the Chinese from invading. But the Tibetans knew they could not resist a Chinese attack for long. At best, Tibet could assemble fewer than ten thousand troops, no match for the mighty Chinese. More than that, as the Dalai Lama wrote years afterward, "the Tibetan army suffered from having few modern weapons and almost no training."[58]

The Chinese conflicts came to a sudden end during the Chinese Revolution of 1949, when the Dalai Lama was just fourteen. That year, all of mainland China became unified under Mao Zedong, the head of China's Communist Party. Mao's ascension to power was deeply disturbing to most Tibetans. The new Chinese leader was determined to add as much territory to China as possible. He was also a brutal warrior, capable of acts of great violence. And as a Communist, he was deeply hostile to religion. As one writer wryly observed, Mao and his Communist Party considered religious

Mao Zedong proclaims the founding of the People's Republic of China in 1949.

organizations "ideological rivals"[59] and aimed to wipe them out.

Invasion

The Tibetans did what they could to stave off an attack. Knowing it would do little good, they mobilized their small army and trained a few more troops. Tibetan diplomats and leaders sought military and diplomatic help from other countries, too, but no one offered assistance. The United States would not meet with the Tibetan delegation, India declined to help for fear of offending China, and the United Nations refused Tibet's request, perhaps in part because Tibet had never joined the organization.

With these avenues cut off, Tibetans turned to their religious roots for assistance. For centuries, Tibetan Buddhism had been at the center of Tibetan life; perhaps prayer and meditation could do what diplomacy and armies could not. Religious festivals became more dramatic and ornate. Lamas read from scripture at daily prayer vigils, and ordinary citizens increased the time and energy they expended on religious rites. "On mountain peaks throughout the land," writes historian Michael Harris Goodman, "incense fires smoldered and prayer wheels revolved with the wind in supplication to the protective deities above."[60]

The Tibetans made one other important change, too. In theory, the young Dalai Lama was not supposed to take over his full duties as priest and temporal leader until he turned eighteen. Until then, other lamas were to be in charge of the country, both spiritually and governmentally. But in 1950, with a crisis looming, the people and leaders of Tibet decided to speed up the process. It was important, they reasoned, for the country to have a strong spiritual leader in a time of danger. Although he was only fifteen, Lhamo was formally enthroned as the Dalai Lama in November 1950.

Unfortunately, nothing could dissuade Mao. In the fall of 1950, Chinese troops entered eastern Tibet with the intention of eventually conquering the entire country. In Mao's words, the soldiers were there to "free Tibetans from imperialist oppression,"[61] meaning the influence of Western non-Communist nations. It was only an excuse; there were virtually no Westerners anywhere in Tibet. Gradually, Chinese soldiers fought their way to Lhasa, the capital. In September 1951, they marched into the city. The conquest of Tibet was complete.

"Religion Is Poison"

Over the next eight years, the Chinese became more and more influential inside Tibet. Their presence was not entirely bad for the Tibetans. The Chinese, for instance, built schools and hospitals where none had previously existed. They also eliminated some of the excesses of Tibet's feudal economic system, in which thousands of poor peasants were constantly in debt to their wealthier landlords.

But in most ways, the Tibetans chafed under Chinese rule. The invaders took Tibetans' lands and possessions, used up Tibetan food supplies, and forced Tibetan peasants to work on various government projects. Loudspeakers in Lhasa and other cities bombarded passersby with Marxist messages. Moreover, Chinese officials persecuted those who spoke out against their policies or whose attitudes marked them as insufficiently Communist.

That was particularly true in the case of religion. Early in the Chinese occupation, the Communist government began dissuading Tibetan Buddhists from practicing their faith. "Why join the monkhood?" asked leaflets encouraging young Buddhist men to choose Marxism over life as a monk. "Why spend your life poring over boring, musty scriptures?"[62] Lamas lost privileges, and religious ceremonies became muted in response to the wishes of the Chinese invaders.

For a time, the Dalai Lama was able to act as a bulwark against the Communist leaders. Recognizing the importance of the Dalai Lama in Tibetan history, the Chinese made little attempt at first to interfere with his authority as the religious leader of Tibet. Instead of treating him with force, they tried to sway him with kindness and argument. In 1954, Mao even hosted the Dalai Lama on a year-long journey to China.

The strategy was very nearly effective. The young Dalai Lama saw much that impressed him. Although he did not agree with many of Mao's tactics, he found himself drawn to some aspects of Communist ideology. "The more I

Accompanied by a Chinese official, the Dalai Lama (third from right) inspects troops in Tibet in 1956. The Dalai Lama initially sought to reconcile Marxist and Buddhist thought.

Religious Oppression in Tibet

Among those Tibetan religious figures imprisoned by the Chinese was the Panchen Lama, a friend of the Dalai Lama and the second most important figure in Tibetan Buddhism. For his refusal to give in to the reigning Communists, he was locked up through most of the 1960s and 1970s. Released in 1977, the Panchen Lama entered a world very different from the one he had known. Once, religion had dominated Tibetan life, and Tibetan culture had flourished. By the time of his release, though, as Isabel Hilton writes in *The Search for the Panchen Lama*,

> All of the hundreds of the monasteries in which he [the Panchen Lama]

had been venerated as a living Buddha were closed, and more had been demolished, stone by stone. In Lhasa, the Jokhang temple, the holiest of all Tibet's holy places, had been sacked and its precious scriptures scattered to the four winds. In Tashilhumpo, his monastery, a third of the buildings had been destroyed. The tombs that had held the bones of his five predecessors had been smashed open and their contents scattered. The Potala, once home to the Dalai Lama, was empty and barricaded, floating above a city from which all traces of colour and joy had been drained.

looked at Marxism, the more I liked it," he remembered later. "Here was a system based on equality and justice for everyone."[63] For a time, the Dalai Lama explored ways in which traditional Buddhism and Marxist thought could complement and support each other.

But in the end, the Dalai Lama rejected the notion that the Chinese brand of communism was compatible with his own religious beliefs. While his appreciation of Marxist principles did not diminish, the Dalai Lama soon came to realize that Mao's application of them was far from acceptable. His last meeting with Mao drove that point home with exceptional clarity. "Religion," Mao informed him, "is poison."[64] As the Dalai Lama described it later, the words sent a shiver of fear down his spine.

The Noose Tightens

Soon after the Dalai Lama returned to Lhasa, the Chinese increased their control over Tibet. They stifled dissent and strengthened their military presence in the capital and elsewhere. Many of their actions were aimed specifically at the Tibetan Buddhist faith. Squadrons of soldiers bombed monasteries, demolished religious objects, and humiliated Tibetans who had taken holy orders. Those who resisted were tortured or killed.

These measures sparked anger and hatred among Tibetans. By 1956, organized guerrilla actions had begun against the occupying Chinese. Tibetan fighters ambushed Chinese soldiers and interfered with Chinese military installations. Chinese authorities acted swiftly to quell the rebellion themselves, torturing guerrillas and innocent people alike in an attempt to intimidate the dissidents. Still, the guerrilla actions did not stop. If anything, the strong Chinese reactions spurred the Tibetans on to further resistance.

In 1958, though, the Chinese government took a new tack. A Chinese official visited the Dalai Lama and insisted that he step forward and stop the guerrilla fighters. As diplomatically as possible, the Dalai Lama refused. While his religious convictions meant that he could not support acts of violence among his people, neither could

he bring himself to criticize their response. The official went away angry. The situation, it was clear, was rapidly growing worse.

"Go! Go! Tonight!"

In March 1959, the Dalai Lama received an invitation from Chinese leaders to attend a dance performance in a Chinese military camp near Lhasa. The invitation requested that the Dalai Lama arrive without his usual assortment of bodyguards. It also demanded that the Dalai Lama keep his attendance at the performance a secret from all but a few Tibetans. Although it seemed like a trap,

The Dalai Lama (left) and another monk confer at a dining table. Some of his most trusted advisers counseled him to refuse an invitation to China in 1959.

the Dalai Lama could not refuse the invitation without causing a severe diplomatic crisis. After meeting briefly with his most trusted advisers, he decided to attend the performance.

Word of his decision, however, quickly leaked out to the general population. Most Tibetans assumed that the invitation was a hoax, a plot to imprison or even murder the Dalai Lama. Many residents of Lhasa gathered outside the Norbulingka, the Dalai Lama's palace. Members of the crowd shouted anti-Chinese slogans. The Chinese, in turn, threatened to fire at the crowd if they did not disperse.

Over the next several days the hostilities escalated while the Dalai Lama watched, in growing alarm, from inside his palace. Twice, following an old Tibetan Buddhist tradition, he consulted an oracle for advice, but the oracle— a spirit inside a medium's body—only counseled him to wait. The Dalai Lama put off the Chinese once or twice, promising to attend the performance as soon as time permitted. Still, he knew he could not do this indefinitely.

Finding the Dalai Lama

Although there are no obvious indications of the new Dalai Lama's identity, Buddhist authorities have developed methods to help them find the next manifestation of Chenrezig. Many of these methods are highly mystical. Search parties may use images from dreams and visions of other lamas, for instance, to give them an idea of where to look. In the case of Lhamo Thondup, for example, a likeness of the boy's family home had appeared in a senior lama's vision. The first task of the search party was to find a house that resembled the one in the vision in as many particulars as possible.

Once a few potential candidates have been located, the searchers usually make use of tests to determine which is the true Dalai Lama. Some of these are physical: The Dalai Lama is said to have distinctive eyes, for example, and unusually large ears, so part of the examination consists of measuring the young candidates' faces.

There are other tests, too, designed to reveal a possible association with former manifestations of Chenrezig. One common tactic is to show a small boy a collection of objects, some of which belonged to an earlier Dalai Lama. A boy who is drawn specifically to those objects may be the next reincarnation of Chenrezig—and therefore, the next Dalai Lama. In contrast, a boy who does not seem able to tell the difference is not the correct choice. Lhamo Thondup, for example, picked out a set of prayer beads, a walking stick, an ivory drum, and several other objects, all of which had belonged to the thirteenth Dalai Lama. None of the other potential candidates picked more than two of the items in question. Lhamo's performance left the search party certain of his true identity.

Hikers trek through the Himalayas. This photo illustrates the great obstacles the Dalai Lama and his group had to face in fleeing Tibet.

On March 17, the Dalai Lama consulted the oracle once more. This time the results were different. As the Dalai Lama explained it later: "To my astonishment [the oracle] shouted, 'Go! Go! Tonight!' The medium, still in his trance, then staggered forward and, snatching up some paper and a pen, wrote down quite clearly and explicitly the route I should take out of the Norbulingka, down to the last Tibetan town on the Indian border."[65] The advice was unexpected, but the message was clear, and the Dalai Lama knew he must act on the oracle's advice. He immediately began making plans to escape to India, letting only a very few trusted advisers in on the secret. Soon after, the Dalai Lama disguised himself, read a few passages from Buddhist scriptures, meditated briefly, and left the building.

Hurrying Toward Freedom

The next few minutes were terrifying for the Dalai Lama. He decided it would be best to remove his glasses, which were unusual in Tibetan society and might make him instantly recognizable. However, he could scarcely see without them. Several assistants, therefore, had to lead him across the courtyard and through the crowd. "I could sense the presence of a great mass of humanity as I stumbled on," he wrote later, "but they did not take any notice of us."[66] That was fortunate. Had the Tibetans recognized him, they might have followed him or insisted on protecting him from the Chinese, with chaos and bloodshed the probable result.

The Dalai Lama had successfully escaped the attention of his own people. The next hurdle would be to evade the Chinese. He was helped in this effort by a quirk of the weather. Sandstorms are common in Lhasa during the late winter, and a particularly violent one sprang up on the night of March 17. At one point the group's path took them within a few hundred yards of a Chinese military camp. But the whirling sand obscured their figures, and the soldiers were busy seeking refuge from the storm. The Dalai Lama passed by without drawing any attention.

Near the edge of Lhasa flowed the Kyichu River, too deep to wade and too dangerous to swim. The Dalai Lama's assistants, however, had already sent word of the escape to trusted Buddhist officials in the area. When the group arrived at the riverbank, they found a group of boats and ferrymen to take them across. "The crossing went smoothly," the Dalai Lama remembered, "although I was certain that every splash of oars would draw down machine-gun fire on us."[67]

Once safely across the Kyichu, the group waited to allow a few other Tibetans to join them. This group included several senior lamas, along with the Dalai Lama's mother, siblings, and former teachers. The Dalai Lama knew that their close relationship to him would probably doom them if they were captured by the Chinese. Delaying the escape on their behalf represented a risk, and the greater numbers made

Tibetan monks surrender to armed Chinese troops. After the Dalai Lama left Lhasa, the Chinese military surrounded the city.

the escape that much more difficult. Still, the Dalai Lama could not imagine fleeing without the people who had been so important in his life.

By this time, the travelers were tired and terrified. But it was essential to press on. Chinese military encampments were all around Lhasa; indeed, one stood just beyond the point at which the party crossed the Kyichu. The farther the travelers could go that night, the safer they would be. Under cover of darkness and blowing sand, they collected a group of ponies from some waiting guerrillas and rode off toward the seventeen-thousand-foot-high pass, Che-la, that led into the next valley to the south.

Che-la and the Tsangpo

Speed was necessary for another reason, too. Although the Chinese army did not know where the travelers were heading, it was easy enough to deduce that their destination was India. Even if Chinese soldiers could not chase them through the higher elevations, there were alternate routes leading to the valley beyond Che-la. It was important to conquer the pass before the Chinese could trace them.

The journey to Che-la was miserable. There were no roads. The winding path up the mountainside was extremely narrow and so steep that the travelers had to lead their horses instead of riding. During the climb, however, an elderly man suddenly appeared with a fresh horse for the Dalai Lama. The travelers considered this a propitious sign. Summoning their strength, they clambered up the path to the top of Che-la. Then they turned back to look upon Lhasa. For many, it would be the last time they would see their capital city.

The other side of Che-la was much less steep, and the group soon came to the Tsangpo River in the valley below. They were pleased to find that they had arrived in advance of the Chinese. Local residents greeted the Dalai Lama and his company with cheers; then they ferried the party across the Tsangpo. They also offered the Dalai Lama the services of about 350 guerrillas who lived in the area. These men were armed, experienced fighters, and they joined the group as bodyguards.

Weary from the journey thus far and reasonably certain that the Chinese would not follow them in the night, the travelers rested that night along the Tsangpo. On the morning of March 19, the group left for their next destination: a fortress called Lhuntse Dzong near the border with India, more than a week's journey away.

To Lhuntse Dzong

South of the Tsangpo, the land grew increasingly barren. Settlements thinned and eventually disappeared altogether. The towering peaks of the Himalayas rose sharply to the sky; even the pass-

Tibetan rebels surrender after two days of fighting the Chinese. Thousands of Tibetans were killed as the Dalai Lama made his way to India.

es between the mountains approached twenty thousand feet. The weather was bitterly cold, and blizzards slowed the pace of the group, making the Dalai Lama worry for his older, less physically fit companions.

As the group traveled deeper into this isolated region, however, they took a certain comfort in the fact that they were not being closely followed. Moreover, they knew that the rugged terrain would make it difficult for the Chinese army to stage a full-fledged pursuit. The greater danger, in fact, was from the air: From time to time, Chinese army planes hummed overhead. But the group split up occasionally to make themselves more difficult to see, and the skies remained overcast through most of the flight south.

Originally, the Dalai Lama had hoped to make contact with the Chinese leaders from Lhuntse Dzong. Once at a safe distance from the commotion of Lhasa, he thought he might be able to reassert his authority over Tibet and to open negotiations with the Chinese. In particular, he hoped to convince the Chinese to leave Lhasa untouched and to ease their oppressive attitudes toward Tibet and Tibetan Buddhism. But about five days after the Dalai Lama left Lhasa, a messenger brought him bad news. The Chinese army had shelled the Norbulingka and machine-gunned thousands of civilians to death.

Upon hearing this information, the Dalai Lama decided that there was no point in trying to negotiate. "From that moment," he wrote later, "it was in-evitable that I should leave my country. There was nothing more I could do for my people if I stayed."[68] Nevertheless, the Dalai Lama pressed on toward the fortress. Once there, he reaffirmed his commitment to serve as Tibet's spiritual and political leader.

The Final Push

Believing that they had outpaced the Chinese, the travelers planned to stay nearly a week at Lhuntse Dzong. They certainly needed the rest; besides, there was every possibility that this stop would be the last taste of Tibetan life for many of the travelers. But on their second day at the fortress, messengers reported the presence of Chinese soldiers in the area. Despite Lhuntse Dzong's fortifications, the Dalai Lama quickly made the decision to move on. "Wherever we tried to stop," he remembered afterward, "the Chinese could hunt us out. . . . My presence there would only lead in the end to more fighting."[69]

Only about 120 miles remained, about half the distance the group had already traveled. But in some ways, this was the most difficult portion of the trip. The horses were exhausted and underfed; the people were not in much better condition. One blizzard after another pummeled the travelers as they made their way south, and the bright light of the sun reflecting off fallen snow blinded them when the blizzards were over. Nor was snow the only problem: A violent dust storm struck one afternoon, and an equally violent rainstorm overtook the group several nights later.

The rainstorm, in fact, almost put a halt to the escape. The Dalai Lama sheltered himself in a tent that night, but the tent leaked. "No matter where I dragged my bedding," he recalled, "I could not escape the water which ran in rivulets down the inside."[70] The cold rain made a low-grade fever worse, and by the next morning the Dalai Lama had a severe case of dysentery.

Ideally, the group would have allowed the Dalai Lama to make a full recovery before pushing on. Unfortunately, even

in this remote mountain region, they were concerned about Chinese troops. The group transferred their leader to a nearby house, where he rested the next day and the following night. Then, despite the Dalai Lama's weakened condition, it was time to move on.

It was March 31, two full weeks after the Dalai Lama had slipped unnoticed out of the palace at Lhasa. The group hurried as quickly as possible along the rocky trails of extreme southern Tibet. When it became clear that there were no Chinese forces nearby,

Hikers backpack across the rugged Himalayas. The Dalai Lama endured blizzards, dust storms, and harsh terrain to escape from the Chinese.

Leader in Exile

Since 1959, China has consistently held power in Tibet, and the Dalai Lama has yet to return to his homeland. He continues to serve as the spiritual leader of his people, though, from his exile in northern India. Over the years, he has acquired a reputation for spirituality and wisdom, and has caught the attention of millions of people, Buddhist and non-Buddhist alike, across the world. In 1989, he was awarded the Nobel Peace Prize for his attempts to find a solution to the conflict in Tibet—and for his work on behalf of peace in other countries as well.

The Dalai Lama continues to hope that someday the Chinese occupation of Tibet will end and that he will be able to return to his country. At the same time, though, he is realistic enough to know that he may live the rest of his life in exile. The Dalai Lama is uncertain whether there will be a fifteenth Dalai Lama after his death. It is possible, he says, that Tibetan Buddhism has been so changed during the last half century that there will no longer be any

The Dalai Lama believes that his successor will come from outside Chinese-occupied Tibet.

use for a supreme leader. But if there is to be a new Dalai Lama, he says, the child will not come from the same place as the previous fourteen. "That [next] reincarnation [of Chenrezig]," he said in 1997, as quoted in Tom Morgan, ed., *A Simple Monk*, "will definitely not come under Chinese control; it will be outside, in the free world. This I can say with absolute certainty."

the guerrilla fighters turned back; they would continue to struggle against the Chinese occupation. The rest of the group soon arrived at the frontier and crossed into India. There they were welcomed by border guards and a government official.

The Dalai Lama, like the other members of his party, was exhausted, weak, and despondent over the conquest of his country by the opposing Chinese. But he had escaped kidnapping, torture, even death at the hands of his persecutors—and he was free.

Appendix

Documents Pertaining to Religious Oppression

The Israelites Depart from Egypt

One of the earliest accounts of escape from religious oppression appears in the Old Testament book of Exodus—a word that means "departure" or "migration." Exodus describes the escape of the Israelites, or Jewish people, from Egypt, where the Pharaoh and his people had enslaved them. The Israelites were under the leadership of Moses, who had received permission from the Pharaoh to lead his people back to the biblical Israel, their homeland. However, as the account describes it, Pharaoh changed his mind soon after the Israelites began their journey.

Some people today believe that the sequence of events as described in Exodus is more literature than history. However, scholars generally agree that the broader story—the enslavement and ultimate escape of the Israelites—is rooted in historical fact. One source, for instance, dates the Exodus to the thirteenth century BC.

1: Then the LORD said to Moses,

2: "Tell the people of Israel to turn back and encamp in front of Pi-ha-hi'roth, between Migdol and the sea, in front of Ba'al-ze'phon; you shall encamp over against it, by the sea.

3: For Pharaoh will say of the people of Israel, 'They are entangled in the land; the wilderness has shut them in.'

4: And I will harden Pharaoh's heart, and he will pursue them and I will get glory over Pharaoh and all his hosts [armies]; and the Egyptians shall know that I am the LORD." And they did so.

5: When the king of Egypt was told that the people had fled, the mind of Pharaoh and his servants was changed toward the people, and they said, "What is this we have done, that we have let Israel go from serving us?"

6: So he [Pharaoh] made ready his chariot and took his army with him,

7: and took six hundred picked [the best] chariots and all the other chariots of Egypt with officers over all of them.

8: And the LORD hardened the heart of Pharaoh king of Egypt and he pursued the people of Israel as they went forth defiantly.

9: The Egyptians pursued them, all Pharaoh's horses and chariots and his horsemen and his army, and overtook them encamped at the sea, by Pi-ha-hi'roth, in front of Ba'al-ze'phon.

10: When Pharaoh drew near, the people of Israel lifted up their eyes, and behold, the Egyptians were marching after them; and they were in great fear. And the people of Israel cried out to the LORD;

11: and they said to Moses, "Is it because there are no graves in Egypt that you have taken us away to die in the wilderness? What have you done to us, in bringing us out of Egypt?

12: Is not this what we said to you in Egypt, 'Let us alone and let us serve the Egyptians'? For it would have been better for us to serve the Egyptians than to die in the wilderness."

13: And Moses said to the people, "Fear not, stand firm, and see the salvation of the LORD, which he will work for you today; for the Egyptians whom you see today, you shall never see again.

14: The LORD will fight for you, and you have only to be still."

15: The LORD said to Moses, "Why do you cry to me? Tell the people of Israel to go forward.

16: Lift up your rod, and stretch out your hand over the sea and divide it, that the people of Israel may go on dry ground through the sea.

17: And I will harden the hearts of the Egyptians so that they shall go in after them, and I will get glory over Pharaoh and all his host, his chariots, and his horsemen.

18: And the Egyptians shall know that I am the LORD, when I have gotten glory over Pharaoh, his chariots, and his horsemen."

19: Then the angel of God who went before the host of Israel moved and went behind them; and the pillar of cloud [a manifestation of God] moved from before them and stood behind them,

20: coming between the host of Egypt and the host of Israel. And there was the cloud and the darkness; and the night passed without one coming near the other all night.

21: Then Moses stretched out his hand over the sea; and the LORD drove the sea back by a strong east wind all night, and made the sea dry land, and the waters were divided.

22: And the people of Israel went into the midst of the sea on dry ground, the waters being a wall to them on their right hand and on their left.

23: The Egyptians pursued, and went in after them into he midst of the sea, all Pharaoh's horses, his chariots, and his horsemen.

24: And in the morning watch the LORD in the pillar of fire and of cloud looked down upon the host of the Egyptians, and discomfited [confused] the host of the Egyptians,

25: clogging their chariot wheels so that they drove heavily; and the Egyptians said, "Let us flee from before Israel; for the LORD fights for them against the Egyptians."

26: The the LORD said to Moses, "Stretch our your hand over the sea, that the water may come back upon the Egyptians, upon their chariots, and upon their horsemen."

27: So Moses stretched forth his hand over the sea, and the sea returned to its wonted [accustomed] flow when the morning appeared; and the Egyptians fled into it, and the LORD routed the Egyptians in the midst of the sea.

28: The waters returned and covered the chariots and the horsemen and all the host of Pharaoh that had followed them into the sea; not so much as one of them remained.

29: But the people of Israel walked on dry ground through the sea, the waters being a wall to them on their right hand and on their left.

30: Thus the LORD saved Israel that day from the hand of the Egyptians; and Israel saw the Egyptians dead upon the seashore.

31: And Israel saw the great work which the LORD did against the Egyptians, and the people feared the LORD; and they believed in the LORD and in his servant Moses.

Revised Standard Version of the Holy Bible, http://etext.lib.virginia.edu.

Muhammad and the Hegira

The Muslim calendar is measured from the hegira, or hejira—the year in which the prophet Muhammad fled from Mecca to Medina. Muhammad, the founder of Islam, was forced to preach and practice his religion mainly in secret. The people of Mecca, where Muhammad lived, viewed the new faith with deep suspicion. That was especially true of believers in the dominant Koreish faith.

The hegira took place in 622 A.D. In this excerpt, author R.F. Dibble describes Muhammad's flight from Mecca with his friend Abu Bekr and eventual arrival in the much more welcoming city of Medina, both in present-day Saudi Arabia. The details of Muhammad's historical escape are somewhat murky, so Dibble relies partly on Islamic tradition in his account.

In the middle of June [Muhammad] received the fearful intelligence [news] that the Koreish intended to visit him. Their purpose is uncertain. It has been surmised [guessed] that they had decided to assassinate him. . . . Tradition states that [the angel] Gabriel informed the Prophet of the malignant design; he at once told [Muhammad's cousin] Ali to lie upon his bed, then went forth, and simultaneously greeted the evil-comers with a handful of dust and this excerpt from the Koran, "And We have covered them so that they shall not see." For, indeed, the best of plotters had wrapped Mohammed in a cloak of invisibility; he therefore escaped undetected while the murderous men lay in wait, thinking that the silent figure on the bed was the Prophet until the morning light apprised them of their sad error. It seems more likely, however, that Mohammed merely threw his deceptive red mantle over the recumbent Ali, and then slipped out of the back window to join the trembling Abu Bekr, who wept joyous tears now that his superior had at last decided to leave Mecca.

For the next three days, the two men lay in concealment in a neighboring cave, while the distracted Koreish feverishly sought everywhere for them. The house of Abu Bekr was searched, but when his daughter Asma was asked, "Where is thy father?" she innocently replied, "Truly, I know not where he is"—whereupon Abu Jahl, a ferocious and impudent fellow, "slapped her on the face with such force that one of her ear-rings dropped." Meanwhile the two outcasts lurked in the secrecy of the cave, across whose entrance, we are informed, a divinely commissioned spider wove a protecting web; yet legends are often more industrious than spiders. Abu Bekr would shake with fear and breathe the low whisper, "What if one were to look through the chink, and see us underneath his very feet?" to which the Prophet would boldly reply: "Think not thus, Abu Bekr! We are two, but God is in the midst a third.". . .

After three days had passed without their detection, it seemed safe to speed toward Medina. The careful Abu Bekr had fetched a purse, bulging with thousands of gold pieces, as well as two of his best camels; and, probably on the night of June 20, they mounted the beasts—Mohammed taking care to choose the swifter one, Al-Kaswa—and started on the perilous journey. The two-hundred-odd miles that they must traverse extended over a parched, barren, inexpressibly desolate and mournful waste, where only such rugged trees as the tamarind and acacia could exist, where phantom mirages mocked the eye, and all nature was but a ribbed and menacing skeleton. They traveled chiefly at night, resting during the sweltering heat of the day and buying provisions from such scattered Bedouins [desert nomads] as they chanced to encounter. Abu Bekr, who was well known to most of these desert dwellers, was frequently asked who his friend was, and he regularly made the answer, "A guide to lead me," while the diplomatic Prophet kept a strict silence.

At length, after eight days of doubt and deprivation, they came in sight of Medina; but the wary Mohammed had no intention of trusting himself to the city before he knew exactly how things lay. "Lead us," he said to the guide, "straight to the Beni Amr at Koba, and draw not yet nigh unto Medina." This overscrupulous vigilance turned out to be unnecessary, for rumors of his approach had set the city agog with delight; and every morning a band of converts and refugees had posted themselves on a hill to watch his arrival. On this morning one of them, catching sight of the travelers as they trudged toward Koba, raised the rapturous shout: "Ho! he has come! he whom we have been looking for has come!" The marvelous news flew from tongue to tongue, and everybody rushed forth to Koba to greet the majestic guest. Even the children cried out: "Here is the Prophet! He is come! He is come!" while a great crowd surged around him and made profound obeisance [bows]. Then Mohammed knew at last that he was safe among friends. He had escaped from Mecca, where the Koreishite swords might have altered the course of events for all time; but the otherwise dull and sluggish Middle Ages were fated to be infinitely enriched by the romantic contest between the Crescent and the Cross [Islam and Christianity]. "Ye people!" he courteously proclaimed, "show your joy by giving your neighbors the salutation of peace; send portions to the poor; bind close the ties of kinsmanship; and offer up your prayers whilst others sleep. Thus ye shall enter Paradise in peace."

R.F. Dibble, *Mohammed.* New York: Viking, 1926.

Fleeing the Chinese

When the Chinese army occupied Tibet in 1950, they executed resistance leaders, ransacked homes, burned religious texts, confiscated private property, and tortured and enslaved Tibetans. It is not surprising, therefore, that those who had an opportunity to flee their homeland took it. Native Tibetan Tenzin Bhagentsang had such an opportunity in 1986, after living for more than twenty years under Chinese oppression. He and his two young cousins fled Lhasa and for the next few weeks walked over some of the world's tallest mountains, sleeping in caves, hiding from soldiers, until they finally reached freedom in Kathmandu, Nepal.

Their journey continued, up and down mountains day after day, sleeping in caves and in the open, always fearing the soldiers would find them. . . .

Some days later, they came upon a narrow foot bridge suspended by chains over a river. Tenzin left his cousins in a cave and approached cautiously, hiding in the brush. It was then he saw a man on the bridge and a guardhouse. Later that night, Tenzin encountered a shepherd who agreed, for pay, to help them cross the bridge.

"He knew when the guards wouldn't be there," Tenzin said. "I had to trust him."

Hiding under the bridge, they watched a man cross with a flashlight and disappear, and then the shepherd said it was time to go. They climbed up the bank and onto the bridge, the shepherd in the lead followed by the two boys and Tenzin in the rear. With every step, the chains rattled, and Tenzin feared they would be discovered. He imagined the pain of bullets in his back.

On the other side, the shepherd motioned what direction the three should go, then disappeared into the darkness. Tenzin isn't sure but he believes at that moment they had entered Nepal, though the danger was not yet behind them.

A day or so later, a man in a uniform and carrying a gun—presumably a Nepalese policeman—confronted them on a path. He spoke an unfamiliar language, but his gestures were clear: If they didn't give him what he wanted, he would send them back to the Chinese side.

They gave him their money, sleeping bags, nearly everything and proceeded. Tenzin knew there was a Tibetan refugee center in Kathmandu, the capital of Nepal. When he would meet people along the path he would ask: "Kathmandu?" And they would point the way.

Eleven days after beginning their walk across the Himalayas, the three boarded a bus in a tiny village, paid the fare with some money Tenzin had hidden in his shoe and rode into Kathmandu.

As he registered at the refugee center, Tenzin noticed a picture on the wall and broke down in tears.

"That was because I was in an office. I was always scared to go into an office and of the officials," he said. "In Tibet you would only go to an office to experience bad things. Yet, there in that office, the Dalai Lama's picture was hanging. I felt I really had arrived at home. I think that is the first time I learned what freedom is."

Pat Shellenbarger, "Local College Student and Former Tibetan Recalls Harrowing Escape Toward Freedom," *Grand Rapids Press*, February 4, 2001, reprinted as "Escape from Tibet: Local College Student Recalls Escape," World Tibet Network News, February 12, 2001. www.tibet.ca.

The Huguenots

The Huguenots were French Protestants who were subjected to frequent persecutions by their nation's Catholic majority. This account describes the escape of some Huguenot children, most likely during the late 1700s. The Dragonnades, mentioned in the excerpt, was a name given to a law according to which Protestants were forced to feed and house the nation's soldiers, or dragoons, at their expense. Most of the proper names in the account are of towns or regions in France.

One of the most distinguished of the refugee paper-manufacturers was Henry de Portal. The Portals were an ancient and noble family in the south of France of Albigeois descent, who stood by the Protestant faith when the reign of terror began in the south of France. During the reign of Louis XVI, Louis de Portal, the father of Henry, was residing at his chateau de la Portalerie, seven leagues [about twenty-one miles] from Bordeaux. To escape the horrors of the Dragonnades, he set out with his wife and five children to take refuge on his estate in the Cevennes. The Dragoons pursued the family to their retreat, overtook them, and cut down the father, mother, and one of the children. They also burned to the ground the house in which they had taken refuge. The remaining four children concealed themselves in an oven outside the building and were thus saved.

The four orphans—three boys and a girl—immediately determined to make for the coast and escape from France by sea. After a long and perilous journey on foot—exhausted by fatigue and wanting food—they at length reached Montauban, where little Pierre, the youngest, fell down fainting with hunger at the door of a baker's shop. The humane baker took up the child and carried him into the house and fed and cherished him. The other three—Henry, William and Mary de Portal—though grieving to leave their brother behind them, again set out on foot and pressed onward to Bordeaux.

They were so fortunate as to secure a passage by a merchant-vessel, on board of which they were shipped, concealed in barrels. They were among the last of the refugees who escaped, previous to the issue of the infamous order to fumigate all departing vessels [light fires aboard the ship so that the smoke would drive out stowaways]; so as to stifle [suffocate] any Protestant refugees who might be concealed in the cargo. The youthful refugees reached Holland where they found friends and foster-parents and were shortly in a position to assert the dignity of their birth [resume their lives as descendants of nobility should]. Miss Portal succeeded in obtaining a situation as governess in the family of the Countess of Finkelstein. She afterwards married M. Lenormant, a refugee settled in Amsterdam, while Henry and William followed the fortunes of the Prince of Orange, accompanying him to England, and established the family of de Portal in that country.

. . . The youngest brother, Pierre de Portal, who had been left fainting at the door of the baker in Montauban, was brought up to manhood by the baker, held to his Protestantism, and eventually set up as a cloth-manufacturer in France. He prospered, married and his sons grew up around him, one of them eventually becoming lord of Penardieres."

David C.A. Agnew, Protestant Exiles from France. NP, 1866.

The Baha'is Flee Iran

The Baha'i faith was founded in 1863 in Iran. It emphasizes the spiritual unity of all religions and all peoples. Despite its goals and its tradition of nonviolence, the Baha'is have suffered in the nation of their founding; since the Islamic Revolution of 1979, those Baha'is who make their homes in Iran have been subjected to legal oppression, torture, and death. Some have escaped to the United States and other nations. This excerpt describes some of their experiences and escapes.

Until the Islamic Revolution of 1979, Z'eheydoon Samali was the director of public welfare for a city in southern Iran. His wife, Shahla, worked for the welfare bureau as a psychologist. Both are Baha'is. When the regime of the Ayatollah Khomeini came to power, the Samalis, and more than 60 other Baha'is in public service in their city, received an ultimatum from the new government: If they wanted to keep their jobs, they must publicly renounce their religion. All but a handful refused.

"It would have been a lie to deny my faith," says Z'eheydoon, who, with his wife and three children, arrived in the United States last summer [1986] after a harrowing escape from Iran. "I wasn't a particularly strong person, and I regretted losing my job after 15 years of service, but I couldn't reject my faith to keep it.". . .

For three years the Samalis drew on their savings in attempts to run a succession of small, unobtrusive businesses, and they watched helplessly as official harassment of their fellow Baha'is steadily increased. In 1983 Z'eheydoon was arrested. "Twenty-two men surrounded our home," Shahla recalls. "They never identified themselves, and at first I thought they were robbers. Then I realized they were Revolutionary Guards sent by the government. They ransacked everything, and then forced us to sign a paper saying that no damage had been done. You can't ask what the charges are. They have the right to just shoot you down."

Z'eheydoon was put on the floor of a car and driven to prison. During the next 13 days he was interrogated 21 times. "They tied my hands behind my back and put my face to the wall," he says. "Someone walked back and forth behind me. He kept trying to make me say that the Baha'is were sending money to Israel to subvert the Iranian government and that the Baha'is were working with the [ultraconservative] Pinochet government in Chile— things like that. I would tell him that the Baha'is were a spiritual community and not a political party, but he kept trying to put words in my mouth. When I gave an answer he didn't like, he would kick me so hard my head hit the wall and bounced back, and then he would shout at me, 'Stand still.' In the end I was so exhausted that I didn't know what I was agreeing to.". . .

The Samalis' experience is not unusual. According to reports from Baha'i refugees, the approximately 270,000 Baha'is who remain in the country (and make up 1 percent of its population) have been subjected to a campaign of institutionalized discrimination, repression and violence that has already brought all formal Baha'i religious and social activity to a halt and has impoverished what was one of the most culturally advanced groups in prerevolutionary Iran. . . .

Baha'i representatives estimate that approximately 30,000 Baha'is have fled Iran, mostly in the months immediately following the Islamic Revolution. The outflow slowed to a trickle when the Khomeini regime ceased issuing exit visas to Baha'is in the early 1980s. In recent years, about 1,000 Baha'is a year have managed to escape across Iran's borders, usually into Pakistan, where about 1,200 are currently being supported by the United Nations High Commission for Refugees. The largest number of Baha'is fleeing Iran have settled in the United States, which has recently granted them refugee status as victims of religious persecution.

Bergus M. Bordewich, "Unholy War: The Persecution of the Baha'is in Iran." *San Francisco Chronicle*, August 2, 1987.

Notes

Chapter 1:
Roger Williams Escapes

1. Quoted in Perry Miller, *Orthodoxy in Massachusetts 1630–1650.* Gloucester, MA: Peter Smith, 1965, p. 18.
2. Quoted in Miller, *Orthodoxy in Massachusetts*, p. 32.
3. Quoted in Edmund J. Carpenter, *Roger Williams.* New York: Grafton Press, 1909, p. xxviii.
4. Quoted in Miller, *Orthodoxy in Massachusetts*, p. 42.
5. Quoted in Miller, *Orthodoxy in Massachusetts*, p. 49.
6. Quoted in James Harvey Robinson, *Readings in European History*, vol. 2. Boston: Ginn, 1906, p. 224.
7. Quoted in James Ernst, *Roger Williams.* New York: Macmillan, 1932, p. 57.
8. Quoted in Ernst, *Roger Williams*, p. 59.
9. Quoted in Irwin H. Polishook, *Roger Williams, John Cotton, and Religious Freedom.* Englewood Cliffs, NJ: Prentice-Hall, 1967, p. 4.
10. Quoted in William G. McLoughlin, *Rhode Island.* New York: W.W. Norton, 1978, p. 6.
11. Quoted in Polishook, *Roger Williams, John Cotton, and Religious Freedom*, p. 8.
12. Quoted in Polishook, *Roger Williams, John Cotton, and Religious Freedom*, p. 18.
13. Quoted in Ernst, *Roger Williams*, p. 154.
14. Quoted in Howard M. Chapin, *Documentary History of Rhode Island.* Providence, RI: Preston and Rounds, 1916, p. 5.
15. Quoted in Chapin, *Documentary History of Rhode Island*, p. 14.
16. Quoted in McLoughlin, *Rhode Island*, p. 9.

Chapter 2:
Escape from Srebrenica

17. Quoted in Joe Sacco, *Safe Area Goradze.* Seattle: Pantagraphics Books, 2000, p. 87.
18. Quoted in Chuck Sudetic, *Blood and Vengeance.* New York: W.W. Norton, 1998, p. 78.

19. Greg Campbell, *The Road to Kosovo.* Boulder, CO: Westview Press, 1999, p. 56.
20. Quoted in Sudetic, *Blood and Vengeance*, p. 281.
21. Quoted in Jan Willem Honig and Norbert Both, *Srebrenica: Record of a War Crime.* New York: Penguin Books, 1996, pp. 52–53.
22. Quoted in Sacco, *Safe Area Goradze*, p. 202.
23. Quoted in Honig and Both, *Srebrenica*, p. 26.
24. Quoted in David Rohde, *Endgame.* New York: Farrar, Straus and Giroux, 1997, p. 203.
25. Quoted in Rohde, *Endgame*, p. 263.
26. Quoted in Honig and Both, *Srebrenica*, p. 62.

Chapter 3:
Leaving the Soviet Union

27. Quoted in Yaacov Ro'i, *The Struggle for Soviet Jewish Emigration 1948–1967.* Cambridge, UK: Cambridge University Press, 1991, p. 419.
28. Quoted in Martin Gilbert, *The Jews of Hope.* New York: Viking Penguin, 1984, p. 6.
29. Quoted in Gilbert, *The Jews of Hope*, p. 177.
30. Yuri Tarnopolsky, *Memories of 1984.* Lanham, MD: University Press of America, 1993, p. 69.
31. Quoted in Ro'i, *The Struggle for Soviet Jewish Emigration*, p. 29.
32. Quoted in Gilbert, *The Jews of Hope*, p. 206.
33. Quoted in Gilbert, *The Jews of Hope*, p. 156.
34. Albert S. Axelrad, *Refusenik: Voices of Struggle and Hope.* Bristol, IN: Wyndham Hall Press, 1987, p. 58.
35. Quoted in Leonard Schroeter, *The Last Exodus.* New York: Universe Books, 1974, p. 81.
36. Quoted in Boris Morozov, *Documents on Soviet Jewish Emigration.* London: Frank Cass, 1999, p. 105.
37. Mark Ya. Azbel, *Refusenik: Trapped in the Soviet Union.* Boston: Houghton Mifflin, 1981, p. 487.
38. Quoted in Gilbert, *The Jews of Hope*, p. 223.

Chapter 4:
The Mormons Move West

39. Quoted in J. Kingston Pierce, "The Death of Joseph Smith." *American History*, December 2001, p. 58.
40. Quoted in Pierce, "The Death of Joseph Smith," p. 58.
41. Quoted in Roger D. Launius and John E. Hallwas, eds., *Kingdom on the Mississippi Revisited.* Urbana: University of Illinois Press, 1996, p. 167.
42. Quoted in Paul Bailey, *The Armies of God.* Garden City, NY: Doubleday, 1968, p. 93.
43. Quoted in Bailey, *The Armies of God*, p. 128.
44. Quoted in Pierce, "The Death of Joseph Smith," p. 59.
45. Quoted in Howard R. Driggs, *Mormon Trail.* Manchester, NH: Clarke Press, 1947, p. 16.

46. Quoted in Carol Cornwall Madsen, *Journey to Zion*. Salt Lake City: Deseret Book Company, 1997, p. 258.

47. William Clayton, *William Clayton's Journal*. New York: Arno Press, 1973, p. 2.

48. Quoted in Madsen, *Journey to Zion*, p. 167.

49. Quoted in Madsen, *Journey to Zion*, p. 158.

50. Clayton, *William Clayton's Journal*, p. 77.

51. Quoted in Donna Toland Smart, ed., *Mormon Midwife*. Logan: Utah State University Press, 1997, p. 44.

52. Quoted in Charles Kelly, ed., *Journals of John D. Lee*. Salt Lake City: University of Utah Press, 1984, p. 17.

53. Quoted in Driggs, *Mormon Trail*, p. 75.

54. Quoted in Smart, ed., *Mormon Midwife*, p. 99.

Chapter 5:
The Flight of the Dalai Lama

55. Quoted in Tom Morgan, ed., *A Simple Monk*. Novato, CA: New World Library, 2001, p. 23.

56. Quoted in Michael Harris Goodman, *The Last Dalai Lama*. Boston: Shambhala, 1968, p. 14.

57. The Dalai Lama, *Freedom in Exile*. New York: HarperCollins, 1990, p. 25.

58. Dalai Lama, *Freedom in Exile*, p. 52.

59. Isabel Hilton, *The Search for the Panchen Lama*. New York: W.W. Norton, 1999, p. 131.

60. Goodman, *The Last Dalai Lama*, p. 147.

61. Quoted in Gill Farrer-Halls, *The World of the Dalai Lama*. Wheaton, IL: Quest Books, 1998, p. 30.

62. Quoted in Goodman, *The Last Dalai Lama*, p. 198.

63. Dalai Lama, *Freedom in Exile*, p. 90.

64. Quoted in Morgan, *A Simple Monk*, p. 104.

65. Quoted in Farrer-Halls, *The World of the Dalai Lama*, p. 80.

66. Dalai Lama, *Freedom in Exile*, p. 138.

67. Dalai Lama, *Freedom in Exile*, p. 139.

68. Quoted in Goodman, *The Last Dalai Lama*, p. 309.

69. Quoted in Goodman, *The Last Dalai Lama*, p. 310.

70. Dalai Lama, *Freedom in Exile*, p. 142.

For Further Reading

Eric Black, *Bosnia: Fractured Region.* Minneapolis: Lerner, 1999. A well-written and informative history of Bosnia and the Yugoslav war. Contains very little about Srebrenica, but includes many interesting photos, many of them in color.

Stephen Currie, *Escapes from Nazi Persecution.* San Diego: Lucent Books, 2004. Describes the escapes of people from Nazi oppression during and before World War II. Several of the stories involve escapes of Jews.

Harvey Fireside and Bryna J. Fireside, *Young People from Bosnia Talk About War.* Springfield, NJ: Enslow, 1996. Interviews and historical background regarding the war in Bosnia.

Joy Hakim, *A History of Us: Making Thirteen Colonies, 1600–1740.* New York: Oxford University Press, 1993. Part of a highly recommended series of history books; this book includes brief but clear information on Roger Williams and Puritanism.

Whitney Stewart, *The 14th Dalai Lama.* Minneapolis: Lerner, 1996. One of the best of the many biographies of the Dalai Lama written for young adults.

Works Consulted

Books

Albert S. Axelrad, *Refusenik: Voices of Struggle and Hope.* Bristol, IN: Wyndham Hall Press, 1987. A short description of the visit of an American rabbi to the Soviet Union in 1978.

Mark Ya. Azbel, *Refusenik: Trapped in the Soviet Union.* Boston: Houghton Mifflin, 1981. The memoir of a Soviet Jewish scientist who was denied permission to emigrate.

Paul Bailey, *The Armies of God.* Garden City, NY: Doubleday, 1968. The early history of the Mormons, including their experiences in Ohio and Missouri as well as their escape from Nauvoo.

Greg Campbell, *The Road to Kosovo.* Boulder, CO: Westview Press, 1999. A journalist who spent time in Bosnia during the Yugoslav war, Campbell describes his adventures in this book.

Edmund J. Carpenter, *Roger Williams.* New York: Grafton Press, 1909. An early biography of Williams, highly biased in Williams's favor but including useful excerpts from his work.

Howard M. Chapin, *Documentary History of Rhode Island.* Providence, RI: Preston and Rounds, 1916. Documents and explanatory material relating to the history of Rhode Island. Includes information on Roger Williams's escape.

William Clayton, *William Clayton's Journal.* New York: Arno Press, 1973. Clayton was a Mormon leader. This is the record of his travels from Nauvoo to Utah in 1846–1847.

Phillip Corwin, *Dubious Mandate.* Durham, NC: Duke University Press, 1999. Corwin, an employee of the United Nations in Bosnia during 1995, presents his reflections on the events of the summer. Includes some information on Srebrenica.

The Dalai Lama, *Freedom in Exile.* New York: HarperCollins, 1990. The autobiography of the Dalai Lama. An engaging book with important information on his escape to India.

Howard R. Driggs, *Mormon Trail.* Manchester, NH: Clarke Press, 1947.

A short history of the Mormon trek westward.

James Ernst, *Roger Williams*. New York: Macmillan, 1932. Dated biography of Williams, including frequent quotations from his writings.

Gill Farrer-Halls, *The World of the Dalai Lama*. Wheaton, IL: Quest Books, 1998. A well-illustrated book about Tibet, the Dalai Lama, and Tibetan Buddhism. Interesting and informative.

Murray Friedman and Albert D. Chernin, eds., *A Second Exodus*. Hanover, NH: Brandeis University Press, 1999. A book of readings about American intervention in the struggle of the Soviet Jews.

Martin Gilbert, *The Jews of Hope*. New York: Viking Penguin, 1984. Gilbert visited the Soviet Union at a time when emigration was extremely difficult. The book is a summary of his discussions with refuseniks.

Michael Harris Goodman, *The Last Dalai Lama*. Boston: Shambhala, 1968. Somewhat out of date by now. Still, this is an exhaustive and exceptionally well-researched biography of the current Dalai Lama.

Isabel Hilton, *The Search for the Panchen Lama*. New York: W.W. Norton, 1999. About the political controversies surrounding the 1995 search for the newest reincarnation of the Panchen Lama, the second leading figure in Tibetan Buddhism.

Jan Willem Honig and Norbert Both, *Srebrenica: Record of a War Crime*. New York: Penguin Books, 1996. An investigation of what happened in Srebrenica, including some eyewitness accounts of the massacres and the escapes.

Charles Kelly, ed., *Journals of John D. Lee*. Salt Lake City: University of Utah Press, 1984. Lee kept a record of his trek from Winter Quarters to Salt Lake City, along with other periods in his life.

Roger D. Launius and John E. Hallwas, eds., *Kingdom on the Mississippi Revisited*. Urbana: University of Illinois Press, 1996. A collection of scholarly writings on the Mormon experience in Nauvoo.

Carol Cornwall Madsen, *Journey to Zion*. Salt Lake City: Deseret Book Company, 1997. A valuable collection of primary source documents relating to the Mormon journey from Nauvoo to Utah. Includes useful background information.

William G. McLoughlin, *Rhode Island*. New York: W.W. Norton, 1978. A short history of Rhode Island, beginning with Roger Williams's escape from Massachusetts.

Florence A. Merriam, *My Summer in a Mormon Village*. Boston: Houghton Mifflin, 1894. Merriam was a non-Mormon who spent a summer in a Utah community dominated by Mormons.

Perry Miller, *Orthodoxy in Massachusetts 1630–1650.* Gloucester, MA: Peter Smith, 1965. A scholarly investigation of the many shades of Puritanism, both in Massachusetts and in England, and their impact.

Tom Morgan, ed., *A Simple Monk.* Novato, CA: New World Library, 2001. Readings about the Dalai Lama's life and work, including his mother's recollections of his birth and childhood. Profusely illustrated.

Boris Morozov, *Documents on Soviet Jewish Emigration.* London: Frank Cass, 1999. Memorandums, letters, and reports regarding the Soviet government and its response to Jewish dissidents. Includes annotations and an introduction.

Thubten Jigme Norbu and Colin M. Turnbull, *Tibet.* New York: Simon and Schuster, 1968. The history of Tibet and Tibetan Buddhism. Norbu is an older brother of the fourteenth Dalai Lama.

Irwin H. Polishook, *Roger Williams, John Cotton, and Religious Freedom.* Englewood Cliffs, NJ: Prentice-Hall, 1967. A book of readings and introductory material relating to Williams's teachings and his escape to Rhode Island.

James Harvey Robinson, *Readings in European History*, vol. 2. Boston: Ginn, 1906. Includes documents and essays relating to the Puritan-Anglican conflict in England.

David Rohde, *Endgame.* New York: Farrar, Straus and Giroux, 1997. A long, detailed description of the events that led up to the fall of Srebrenica, the massacres, and the aftermath. Well written and informative.

Yaacov Ro'i, *The Struggle for Soviet Jewish Emigration 1948–1967.* Cambridge, UK: Cambridge University Press, 1991. A thorough, well-researched account of the refuseniks during twenty pivotal years.

Joe Sacco, *Safe Area Goradze.* Seattle: Pantagraphics Books, 2000. Sacco spent four years in eastern Bosnia interviewing people and observing the events around him. The book describes the history of the war in Bosnia in the form of a narrative cartoon.

Leonard Schroeter, *The Last Exodus.* New York: Universe Books, 1974. Interviews and information about the lives and hardships of refuseniks, with historical information included.

Donna Toland Smart, ed., *Mormon Midwife.* Logan: Utah State University Press, 1997. Patty Sessions was a Mormon who left Nauvoo in February 1846. Her diary covers the journey to Winter Quarters and then to Utah, continuing until 1888.

Chuck Sudetic, *Blood and Vengeance.* New York: W.W. Norton, 1998. A description of one family's experience of the Bosnian war. Includes information about Srebrenica, along with valuable background.

Yuri Tarnopolsky, *Memories of 1984.* Lanham, MD: University Press of America, 1993. Tarnopolsky was a refusenik who emigrated in 1987 after several years in Soviet prison camps. This is his memoir.

Periodicals

J. Kingston Pierce, "The Death of Joseph Smith." *American History*, December 2001.

David Van Biema, "The Invasion of the Latter-Day Saints." *Time*, July 10, 2003.

Index

Picture Credits

About the Author

Stephen Currie is the creator of Lucent's Great Escapes series. He has also written many other books for children and young adults, among them *Life in the Trenches* and *Terrorists and Terrorist Groups*, both for Lucent. He lives in New York State with his wife and children. Among his hobbies are kayaking, snowshoeing, and bicycling.